The Essential Rilke

The Essential Rilke

REVISED EDITION

SELECTED *and* TRANSLATED *by*

GALWAY KINNELL

and

HANNAH LIEBMANN

THE ECCO PRESS
An Imprint of HarperCollins*Publishers*

HarperCollins books may be purchased for educational, business, or sales promotional use. For information please write: Special Markets Department, HarperCollins Publishers, Inc., 10 East 53rd Street, New York, NY 10022.

First paperback edition published 2000.

The Library of Congress has catalogued the hardcover edition as follows

Rilke, Rainer Maria, 1875–1926.
    [Poems. English & German. Selections]
    The essential Rilke / selected and translated by Galway Kinnell and Hannah Liebmann.—1st ed.
        p. cm.
    ISBN 0-06-095654-2
    1. Rilke, Rainer Maria 1875–1926—Translations into English.   I.
Kinnell, Galway, 1927– II. Liebmann, Hannah, 1933–   III. Title
    PT2635.I65K56   2000
    831'.912—dc21   00-024289

00 01 02 03 04 RRD 10 9 8 7 6 5 4 3 2

To

Silvia Beier
Gilbert Meyns
and C. K. Williams

i fabbri molto miglori

CONTENTS

UNCOLLECTED

DUINO ELEGIES (1923)

from THE SONNETS TO ORPHEUS (1923)

INTRODUCTION

The wish to translate Rilke's poetry first came to me in 1948, when I read all the way through J. B. Leishman and Stephen Spender's exuberant translation of the *Duino Elegies* while standing in the poetry section of the old Eighth Street Bookstore in New York. Even in that first spellbound encounter, I thought I sensed under the words of the translation another, truer Rilke struggling to speak. Possibly many young poets, on first reading the *Elegies,* have had a similar reaction and felt the same impulse to translate. Perhaps the intimacy of Rilke's voice makes it seem that he speaks to you alone and that only you understand him. Perhaps the elusiveness of his poetry makes reading Rilke a more creative act than with most poets, and the poem you come away with, more than usually your own. Based on the large number of English versions of Rilke in bookstores, I have to think that a good number of those early smitten carried through on that wish to translate.

The problem for me was my deficiency in the language. Of course, I noticed an instance or two of collaboration, in which a poet innocent of the language teams up with someone expert in it. As a persnickety constructionist in this matter, I felt that in such an arrangement the amount of knowledge needed was far greater than the person who knew the language could possibly convey to the person who didn't.

Times change, however, bringing new tricks — including many new instances of translation by collaboration — and sometimes even the most recalcitrant old dog will break into a trot and try to catch up. A year ago, seeking someone who might help me understand a certain poem by Rilke, I was put in touch with Hannah Liebmann, a native-speaker of German, utterly fluent in English, and a lover of Rilke's poetry. In our first conversation, a long one that took place over the telephone, Hannah and I seemed linked by some special Pacific Bell neuron connector. We arrived rather easily at an English version; moreover, it looked good to us, almost like a true translation. (A momentary effect: translations have a way of deteriorating when left out in the air even overnight.) Suddenly the idea of collaborating on a selection of Rilke's poems seemed irresistibly appealing; very soon I found myself ascribing to myself, without the least sense of misappropriation, the honorable title of co-translator.

As our book would be bilingual, the selection of poems had to be small—more "quintessential" than *Essential*. Left out are a number of splendid, obviously essential poems, as well as many less familiar ones we would have liked to include.

Early work and poems written in French apart, Rilke wrote poems of five distinct kinds. The first is his *Dinggedichte*, or thing poems. Under the influence of the sculptor Rodin (for whom Rilke worked as secretary for a while), Rilke put aside the direct expression of feeling and conceived of these poems as literary equivalents of sculptural objects. They are, of course, at least the finest of them, saturated in human feeling. For example, "The Panther," which seems almost to have been composed from within the caged animal, is palpably filled with Rilke's sense of being caged himself, in an empathetic self-identification that gives Rilke's voice in the poem its peculiar authority.

The second kind of poem, the elegy—in its modern sense of a lament for the dead—has three exemplars. We include the brilliant "Requiem for a Friend," Rilke's monologue to the ghost of the painter Paula Modersohn-Becker.

This poem is so direct in its address to its subject that the reader is like an eavesdropper—there is none of the artificially conveyed anecdotal background that a reader would find useful. The bare facts are: Several years after her marriage in 1901 to Otto Modersohn, also a painter, Paula Becker left him and went to Paris to devote herself to her painting. There she and Rilke met frequently—every day, during the time she was painting his portrait. In "Requiem for a Friend" Rilke makes reference to a painting of Becker's he was particularly drawn to, done from a photograph she took of herself in a mirror, "Self-Portrait as Half-Nude with Amber Necklace." Then abruptly, for unknown reasons, Rilke broke off the sittings and thereafter kept his distance. Eventually, Becker reconciled with Modersohn, became pregnant, and, three weeks after giving birth to a baby girl, died of an embolism.*

"Requiem for a Friend" is an extended meditation on a conundrum that was much on Rilke's mind:

> For somewhere an ancient enmity exists
> between our life and the great works we do.

More than that, it is the anomaly in the corpus of Rilke's work, a poem that focuses fully on a fellow artist whom he regards as an equal. The linguistic stylization attenuates, and we hear Rilke speaking more quietly and intimately and with more feeling than in any other poem.

Representing the third kind of poem is Rilke's major work, the *Duino Elegies*. In a time dominated by anthropomorphic religion, empirical science, and swiftly accelerating technology, the *Duino Elegies* takes up these elemental questions: Who

---

* For full accounts of these circumstances the reader might consult Eric Torgersen's *Dear Friend* (1998), Ralph Freedman's *Life of a Poet: Rainer Maria Rilke* (1996), or Wolfgang Leppman's *Rilke: A Life* (1984).

are we? Where are we? What are our connections with the unknown spaces around us, with the other living beings, and with things? What is our task here? In a way the *Elegies* is a poem that speaks to the most ancient poetic preoccupations.

At the same time, the poem exemplifies Rimbaud's injunction in *A Season in Hell*: "It is necessary to be absolutely modern." It is a collection of ten "intimate immensities"—the phrase is Gaston Bachelard's—which together would form a metaphysics of consciousness, or a tract on a religion of consciousness, were it not so firmly a poem, with all its elements inextricably rooted in images, symbols, events, and situations. In the *Elegies* it is as if like a painter with laden brush he applies language in bold, rapid gestures, sometimes creating abstract constructions that are tantalizingly figurative, sometimes figurative forms that, on being stared at, fall back into the abstract. Often words are organized as if their aural values were primary, forming groups of inter-echoing sounds that can deeply affect us but, as far as meaning goes, remain hard to grasp, as were the once-unintelligible but even then thrilling clusters of sounds in the slow movements of Beethoven's late quartets.

A number of readers and critics have found the early elegies somewhat troubling, particularly on the subject of love. These readers reverse the conventional wisdom—that an artist's human deficiencies, as well as any attendant human wreckage the artist might leave behind, are simply the price that must be paid for great art—and find that certain often-dismissed human flaws in fact damage the art. These more skeptical readers see Rilke less as an authority on how to live than as a sufferer telling in brilliant confusion his own strange and gripping interpretation of what it is to be human.

Others, of course, read the *Elegies* very differently. Some believe that Rilke was not naive about his failure as a lover and see that the first three elegies are attempts to clarify certain difficult truths: that the other is fundamentally unreachable; that the love relationship is often a self-enclosed mutual dependency that cuts off both lovers from what is around and beyond them; that, in loving, the angel and the "river god of the blood" play sometimes clashing roles; and that in our confused modern culture, when earthly divinities have finally been exorcised, no one knows what love is.

Much of the *Duino Elegies* was composed in two great surges of creative activity possibly unmatched in all of poetry. The *Elegies* was started in dramatic fashion in 1912, at the castle at Duino on the Adriatic. By then Rilke was already ensnared in his so-called "crisis years" of "wandering and waiting," often depressed, feeling unable to write—a time of trial that did not end until the second great surge, in 1922, at the Chateau de Muzot in Switzerland. It may be that he was then able to finish his great work because he had recognized his human limitations and, unable or unwilling to change, had come to accept them. It may be, also, that he had been humbled and changed by the First World War—which he at first welcomed, as an opportunity for communal sacrifice, but which soon aroused in him only revulsion. Somehow at last he succeeded in bringing the desperate, desolate voice of the early elegies into the great and serene hymns to the here and now of the ninth and tenth elegies.

This second surge brought with it an "overflow," in the form of a fourth kind of poem, *The Sonnets to Orpheus*, fifty-five poems mostly of reconciliation and praise. During the weeks surrounding the finishing of the *Duino Elegies*, Rilke was in a state of such creative grace that it seemed anything that caught his attention, crossed his mind, or rose out of his memory he could transform almost instantly into a rhymed and metered sonnet needing little or no revision. The outpouring suggests a clearing out of corners of his mind still crowded with thoughts, inklings, wonderments, knowings, in order that he might die—his death would come in 1926, of leukemia—unencumbered by the unsaid.

The fifth category of poem consists simply of all his poems, "pieces" might be a better word, that he did not collect into a book. They include notes, fragments, poems he was not stirred to work on, poems of a bitterness that perhaps he did not want others to see, epistles, dedicatory items, and so forth; a large number of them, from our perspective, are true poems. Rilke had kept writing even when he felt blocked, even when he believed that what he wrote was of no importance. He was a poet driven by periodic passions to compose a great work; and it was this love of the process itself of writing, this natural faithfulness to his art, that kept him, during the often long meanwhiles, in a state of readiness.

When Hannah and I started our project, I knew Rilke mostly through translations, which inevitably smooth out and simplify. Very soon I encountered the intractable and untranslatable Rilke, and I was shocked. Hannah, knowing Rilke in the original, was better prepared, but even she, perhaps accustomed to absorbing the gist of difficult passages by means of her powerful intuition, may have been surprised at how hard it was, as we set about translating, to answer the question put repeatedly by our very practical (but no less beautiful on that account) English language: "It *sounds* splendid but—what exactly is it saying?"

Many of our difficulties came from Rilke's practice of altering conventions of language whenever it suits him. He might take a word or combination of words and change a part of it in a way that inverts the meaning. Because in German complex abstract words are often formed by joining together two or more concrete words, opportunities for inventing words abound. But, while both the way a word was invented and its startling effect are very much part of its value in Rilke's poems, a translator can seldom imitate Rilke's subversions of German formations—and have them sound like English.

Also, Rilke uses certain parts of speech almost interchangeably. He exhumes etymological meanings and sets them against evolved meanings. And it is not always clear what his neologisms mean.

Often in these difficult moments Hannah and I felt we knew (sort of) what Rilke was after; the problem was how to clarify and translate it. In other moments, however, we knew we simply didn't know. Hannah could read a passage in the *Elegies* and feel satisfied that she had grasped it completely, only, on a second reading, to discover that it also had a different or even opposite meaning. Sometimes a line seemed to lie there like a row of lumps of meaning, leaving it to the reader to puzzle out what combination(s) might form a meaning consistent with the context.

Compounding our difficulties was, I'm afraid, my own deficiency in the German language. I came to see that my earlier distrust of translation by collaboration had much justification, at least if the work to be translated has many linguistic irregularities. The partner who knows the language bears too great a burden in figuring out the original, and in explaining it adequately to the partner who doesn't. As the ignorant partner, I sometimes felt I was in a darkened room, trying to imagine, on the basis of verbal descriptions, what I would see from the window if I only knew how to raise the blind.

(I may seem to complain, but in fact it has been a continual pleasure to watch many of Rilke's lines, which I thought we had already squeezed all the meaning out of, repeatedly reveal—in Melville's term—a "little lower layer." And it has been gratifying to me to carry out this long-lurking ambition, for I feel the truth of the observation that Browning ought to have gone on to make: "A man's uncompleted projects shouldn't exceed by too many his completed projects—or what's a hell for.")

Now, this was our plight. What to do? We had already consulted the translators who had gone before us. Few would venture into the Rilkean Bermuda Triangle without first poring over the charts of those who had successfully traversed these treacherous waters—or without inspecting any flotsam for clues to prior sinkings. They were to us a group of friendly experts permanently convened around a seminar table, to whom we could go at any time for help. Having quickly familiarized ourselves with the particular genius of each, we could turn to this one or that as needed. Now they all seem to us like old friends, in admittedly lopsided friendships—except, of course, for those who actually are old friends.

The translators around our imaginary table were Walter Arndt, Robert Bly, Elaine Boney, Patrick Bridgwater, Patricia Brodsky, Leonard Forster, Stephen Garmey, Michael Hamburger, J. B. Leishman, Rika Lesser, Stephen Mitchell, M. D. Herter Norton, Al Poulin Jr., Adrienne Rich, Edward Snow, Stephen Spender, Eric Torgersen, Jay Wilson, Franz Wright, and David Young. I liked how gracious each was in thanking the others, especially the doubly gracious Edward Snow, who in his introduction to his translation of *New Poems* addressed past and then future translators: "For occasionally adopting a reading that a poem seemed absolutely to require, I beg forgiveness; I hope that whoever comes after me will find something worth taking from this volume." We, in turn, when desperate, reached to Snow or another for that absolutely indispensable insight—a right of pilferage, which, should a later translator covet a word in these translations, we gladly pass on. It was as it should be: our talents pressed into the service of some cumulative project more urgent than any of our individual efforts.

But we also needed the active and specific help of experts—experts in German, in Rilke, and in the two together. Our consultations were extensive. The title page of this book might accurately read: "Translated by Galway Kinnell and Hannah Liebmann et al." (Responsibility for errors and misreadings, needless to say, rests with Hannah and me.)

Among these, I want to remember in particular my late dear friend Marion Magid, who fifteen years ago sat with me and made a translation of "Autumn Day." I could almost see her going from the original language to the mind and from the mind to the new language. She also instructed me in the virtue of an occasional small interpolation when a higher fidelity was at stake.

Hannah and I also thank the following people for the help they gave us in so many different ways: Anne Allen, Judy Capodanno, Julie Carr, Julie Cooper, Daniel Halpern, Bernd Hüppauf, my beloved daughter, Maud Kozodoy, and her husband, Neal Kozodoy, Lilach Lachmann, Peter Matson, Margaret Robinson, Ilse Schreiber, Eva-Maria Simms, and Eric Torgersen.

Three of the people who helped us are unmentioned in this list, because our debt to them is so immense. Silvia Beier's glad attention to our project was very heartening, especially coming as it did somewhat late in the work; with her fine sense of the nuances of the idioms of each language, she tried to keep us close to the German and yet not too far from spoken English. Gilbert Meyns, an Australian very much at home in German, who often struck me as having a Rilkean set to his mind (but no doubt it is simply an exceptionally searching and original intelligence), was able to see into many obscure passages, and has, as well, a lively instinct for the English phrase. My old and dear friend, the poet C. K. Williams, with his great gifts of mind and language, found many ways to illuminate and deepen the sense of our translation as well as to enliven its language. It has occurred to me that in an ideal world, Silvia Beier, Gilbert Meyns, and C. K. Williams would have found one another and worked together to produce a version that would have set a new and high standard for Rilke translations. In dedicating this book to them, Hannah and I wish to pay homage to their extraordinary capabilities and their generosity.

Galway Kinnell
Sheffield, Vermont
May 20, 1999

Note to the Revised Edition

Talking with Stanley Kunitz this fall, I bewailed the fact that, because our translation of Rilke had taken so long, Hannah Liebmann and I had been unable to give ourselves a quiet period to "observe" (Rilke's word) the translation before it went to press. In the months since its hardcover publication, in August, we had found ourselves still "observing" in spite of our best efforts to put the work to rest. Stanley said, "Don't worry. Enter your corrections in the paperback edition. There we often find the version that's closest to the translator's heart."

Galway Kinnell
November 30, 1999

from THE BOOK OF IMAGES

AUS EINER KINDHEIT

Das Dunkeln war wie Reichtum in dem Raume,
darin der Knabe, sehr verheimlicht, saß.
Und als die Mutter eintrat wie im Traume,
erzitterte im stillen Schrank ein Glas.
Sie fühlte, wie das Zimmer sie verriet,
und küßte ihren Knaben: Bist du hier? . . .
Dann schauten beide bang nach dem Klavier,
denn manchen Abend hatte sie ein Lied,
darin das Kind sich seltsam tief verfing.

Es saß sehr still. Sein großes Schauen hing
an ihrer Hand, die ganz gebeugt vom Ringe,
als ob sie schwer in Schneewehn ginge,
über die weißen Tasten ging.

FROM A CHILDHOOD

The darkening was like riches in the room
in which the boy sat, quite hidden from sight.
And when his mother entered, as in a dream,
a glass trembled in the quiet cupboard.
She felt how the room betrayed her,
and she kissed the boy: "Oh, you're here? . . ."
Then both looked fearfully at the piano,
because some evenings she'd play the child a song
in which he found himself strangely deeply caught.

He sat very still. His great gaze hung
on her hand, weighed down by its ring,
as if struggling through drifted snow
it went over the white keys.

HERBSTTAG

Herr: es ist Zeit. Der Sommer war sehr groß.
Leg deinen Schatten auf die Sonnenuhren,
und auf den Fluren laß die Winde los.

Befiehl den letzten Früchten voll zu sein;
gieb ihnen noch zwei südlichere Tage,
dränge sie zur Vollendung hin und jage
die letzte Süße in den schweren Wein.

Wer jetzt kein Haus hat, baut sich keines mehr.
Wer jetzt allein ist, wird es lange bleiben,
wird wachen, lesen, lange Briefe schreiben
und wird in den Alleen hin und her
unruhig wandern, wenn die Blätter treiben.

AUTUMN DAY

Lord: it is time. The summer was so immen[
Lay your shadow on the sundials,
and let loose the wind in the fields.

Bid the last fruits to be full;
give them another two more southerly days,
press them to ripeness, and chase
the last sweetness into the heavy wine.

Whoever has no house now will not build one anymore.
Whoever is alone now will remain so for a long time,
will stay up, read, write long letters,
and wander the avenues, up and down,
restlessly, while the leaves are blowing.

DAS LIED DES BETTLERS

Ich gehe immer von Tor zu Tor,
verregnet und verbrannt;
auf einmal leg ich mein rechtes Ohr
in meine rechte Hand.
Dann kommt mir meine Stimme vor
als hätt ich sie nie gekannt.

Dann weiß ich nicht sicher wer da schreit,
ich oder irgendwer.
Ich schreie um eine Kleinigkeit.
Die Dichter schrein um mehr.

Und endlich mach ich noch mein Gesicht
mit beiden Augen zu;
wie's dann in der Hand liegt mit seinem Gewicht
sieht es fast aus wie Ruh.
Damit sie nicht meinen ich hätte nicht,
wohin ich mein Haupt tu.

THE BEGGAR'S SONG

Always I go from gate to gate,
rained on, scorched by the sun;
suddenly I press my right ear
into my right hand.
And now my own voice comes to me
as if I'd never known it.

So that I'm not certain who's crying out,
I or someone else.
I cry for a pittance.
The poets cry for more.

At last I close my face
by closing both my eyes;
lying so heavy in my hand
it almost looks like rest.
So they won't think I hadn't
a place to lay my head.

from NEW POEMS

PIETÀ

So seh ich, Jesus, deine Füße wieder,
die damals eines Jünglings Füße waren,
da ich sie bang entkleidete und wusch;
wie standen sie verwirrt in meinen Haaren
und wie ein weißes Wild im Dornenbusch.

So seh ich deine niegeliebten Glieder
zum erstenmal in dieser Liebesnacht.
Wir legten uns noch nie zusammen nieder,
und nun wird nur bewundert und gewacht.

Doch, siehe, deine Hände sind zerrissen—:
Geliebter, nicht von mir, von meinen Bissen.
Dein Herz steht offen und man kann hinein:
das hätte dürfen nur mein Eingang sein.

Nun bist du müde, und dein müder Mund
hat keine Lust zu meinem wehen Munde—.
O Jesus, Jesus, wann war unsre Stunde?
Wie gehn wir beide wunderlich zugrund.

PIETÀ

And so I see your feet again, Jesus,
which then were the feet of a young man
when shyly I undressed them and washed them;
how they were entangled in my hair,
like white deer in the thornbush.

And I see your never-loved limbs
for the first time, in this night of love.
We never lay down together
and now we have only adoring and watching over.

But look, your hands are torn—:
beloved, not from me, not from any bites of mine.
Your heart is open and anyone can enter:
It should have been the way in for me alone.

Now you are tired, and your tired mouth
has no desire for my aching mouth—.
O Jesus, Jesus, when was our hour?
How we both wondrously perish.

DER PANTHER
Im Jardin des Plantes, Paris

Sein Blick ist vom Vorübergehn der Stäbe
so müd geworden, daß er nichts mehr hält.
Ihm ist, als ob es tausend Stäbe gäbe
und hinter tausend Stäben keine Welt.

Der weiche Gang geschmeidig starker Schritte,
der sich im allerkleinsten Kreise dreht,
ist wie ein Tanz von Kraft um eine Mitte,
in der betäubt ein großer Wille steht.

Nur manchmal schiebt der Vorhang der Pupille
sich lautlos auf—. Dann geht ein Bild hinein,
geht durch der Glieder angespannte Stille—
und hört im Herzen auf zu sein.

THE PANTHER
In the Jardin des Plantes, Paris

His gaze has grown so tired from the bars
passing, it can't hold anything anymore.
It is as if there were a thousand bars
and behind a thousand bars nothing.

The soft gait of powerful supple strides,
which turns in the smallest of all circles,
is like a dance of strength around a center
where an imperious will stands stunned.

Only at times the curtain of the pupils
silently opens—. Then an image enters,
passes through the taut stillness of the limbs—
and in the heart ceases to be.

DER SCHWAN

Diese Mühsal, durch noch Ungetanes
schwer und wie gebunden hinzugehn,
gleicht dem ungeschaffnen Gang des Schwanes.

Und das Sterben, dieses Nichtmehrfassen
jenes Grunds, auf dem wir täglich stehn,
seinem ängstlichen Sich-Niederlassen—:

in die Wasser, die ihn sanft empfangen
und die sich, wie glücklich und vergangen,
unter ihm zurückziehn, Flut um Flut;
während er unendlich still und sicher
immer mündiger und königlicher
und gelassener zu ziehn geruht.

THE SWAN

This drudgery of trudging through tasks
yet undone, heavily, as if bound,
is like the swan's not fully created walking.

And dying, this no longer being able
to hold to the ground we stand on every day,
like the swan's anxious letting himself down—:

into the waters, which gently accept him
and, as if happy and already in the past,
draw away under him, ripple upon ripple,
while he, now utterly quiet and sure
and ever more mature and regal
and composed, is pleased to glide.

DIE ERBLINDENDE

Sie saß so wie die anderen beim Tee.
Mir war zuerst, als ob sie ihre Tasse
ein wenig anders als die andern fasse.
Sie lächelte einmal. Es tat fast weh.

Und als man schließlich sich erhob und sprach
und langsam und wie es der Zufall brachte
durch viele Zimmer ging (man sprach und lachte),
da sah ich sie. Sie ging den andern nach,

verhalten, so wie eine, welche gleich
wird singen müssen und vor vielen Leuten;
auf ihren hellen Augen die sich freuten
war Licht von außen wie auf einem Teich.

Sie folgte langsam und sie brauchte lang
als wäre etwas noch nicht überstiegen;
und doch: als ob, nach einem Übergang,
sie nicht mehr gehen würde, sondern fliegen.

GOING BLIND

She sat much like the others at tea.
At first it was as if she held her cup
a little differently from the rest.
She gave a smile. It almost hurt.

And when the time came to rise and talk
and slowly, in no special order,
pass through many rooms (talking and laughing),
then I saw her. She came behind the others,

seeming subdued, like someone who soon
will have to sing before many people;
on her pale eyes full of joy,
light fell from outside, as on a pond.

She followed slowly, taking a long time,
as though something hadn't yet been surmounted;
and yet: as if, as soon as she was past it,
she would no longer walk, but fly.

ORPHEUS . EURYDIKE . HERMES

Das war der Seelen wunderliches Bergwerk.
Wie stille Silbererze gingen sie
als Adern durch sein Dunkel. Zwischen Wurzeln
entsprang das Blut, das fortgeht zu den Menschen,
und schwer wie Porphyr sah es aus im Dunkel.
Sonst war nichts Rotes.

Felsen waren da
und wesenlose Wälder. Brücken über Leeres
und jener große graue blinde Teich,
der über seinem fernen Grunde hing
wie Regenhimmel über einer Landschaft.
Und zwischen Wiesen, sanft und voller Langmut,
erschien des einen Weges blasser Streifen,
wie eine lange Bleiche hingelegt.

Und dieses einen Weges kamen sie.

Voran der schlanke Mann im blauen Mantel,
der stumm und ungeduldig vor sich aussah.
Ohne zu kauen fraß sein Schritt den Weg
in großen Bissen; seine Hände hingen
schwer und verschlossen aus dem Fall der Falten
und wußten nicht mehr von der leichten Leier,
die in die Linke eingewachsen war
wie Rosenranken in den Ast des Ölbaums.
Und seine Sinne waren wie entzweit:
indes der Blick ihm wie ein Hund vorauslief,
umkehrte, kam und immer wieder weit
und wartend an der nächsten Wendung stand,—

ORPHEUS . EURYDICE . HERMES

Here was the wondrous mine of souls.
Like silent silver ore they moved
in veins through its darkness. Among roots
the blood welled up that flows to the humans,
seeming as heavy as porphyry in the dark.
Nothing else was red.

There were rocks
and spectral forests. Bridges across emptiness
and that broad gray blind pond
suspended above its distant bottom
like a rainy sky above a landscape.
And between gentle, forbearing meadows,
appeared the pale strip of the single path,
laid out like a long bleaching place.

And up this one path they came.

In front, the slender man in the blue cloak,
who gazed out ahead, silent, impatient.
His steps devoured the path in giant bites,
not bothering to chew; from the folds of his cloak,
his hands hung down heavy and locked shut,
oblivious to the now weightless lyre
which had grown into his left arm
as tendrils of a rosebush into an olive bough.
His senses were as if split in two:
while his gaze, like a dog, ran out ahead,
turned, came back, and again and again, far
and waiting, stood at the next bend,—

blieb sein Gehör wie ein Geruch zurück.
Manchmal erschien es ihm als reichte es
bis an das Gehen jener beiden andern,
die folgen sollten diesen ganzen Aufstieg.
Dann wieder wars nur seines Steigens Nachklang
und seines Mantels Wind was hinter ihm war.
Er aber sagte sich, sie kämen doch;
sagte es laut und hörte sich verhallen.
Sie kämen doch, nur wärens zwei
die furchtbar leise gingen. Dürfte er
sich einmal wenden (wäre das Zurückschaun
nicht die Zersetzung dieses ganzen Werkes,
das erst vollbracht wird), müßte er sie sehen,
die beiden Leisen, die ihm schweigend nachgehn:

Den Gott des Ganges und der weiten Botschaft,
die Reisehaube über hellen Augen,
den schlanken Stab hertragend vor dem Leibe
und flügelschlagend an den Fußgelenken;
und seiner linken Hand gegeben: *sie.*

Die So-geliebte, daß aus einer Leier
mehr Klage kam als je aus Klagefrauen;
daß eine Welt aus Klage ward, in der
alles noch einmal da war: Wald und Tal
und Weg und Ortschaft, Feld und Fluß und Tier;
und daß um diese Klage-Welt, ganz so
wie um die andre Erde, eine Sonne
und ein gestirnter stiller Himmel ging,
ein Klage-Himmel mit entstellten Sternen—:
Diese So-geliebte.

his hearing lagged behind like a smell.
At times it seemed to him to reach
back to the sounds of walking of the two others
supposed to be following him this whole ascent.
And then again, it was only his own steps' echoes
and the wind stirring his cloak that were behind him.
But he told himself they were still coming;
said it aloud and heard his tones die away.
They were still coming, it was just that they
walked so terribly quietly. If only he
could turn around just once (if looking back
wouldn't subvert the whole undertaking,
not yet completed), he would have to see them,
those two soft walkers following without a word:

The god of the way and of tidings from afar,
a wide brim above his bright eyes,
his slender wand held out in front,
beating wings at his ankles;
and, entrusted to his left hand: *she*.

The one so loved that a single lyre
raised more lament than lamenting women ever did;
and that from the lament a world arose in which
everything was there again: woods and valley
and path and village, field and river and animal;
and around this lament-world, just as
around the other earth, a sun
and a starry silent heaven turned,
a lament-heaven of disordered stars—:
This one so loved.

Sie aber ging an jenes Gottes Hand,
den Schritt beschränkt von langen Leichenbändern,
unsicher, sanft und ohne Ungeduld.
Sie war in sich, wie Eine hoher Hoffnung,
und dachte nicht des Mannes, der voranging,
und nicht des Weges, der ins Leben aufstieg.
Sie war in sich. Und ihr Gestorbensein
erfüllte sie wie Fülle.
Wie eine Frucht von Süßigkeit und Dunkel
so war sie voll von ihrem großen Tode,
der also neu war, daß sie nichts begriff.

Sie war in einem neuen Mädchentum
und unberührbar; ihr Geschlecht war zu
wie eine junge Blume gegen Abend,
und ihre Hände waren der Vermählung
so sehr entwöhnt, daß selbst des leichten Gottes
unendlich leise, leitende Berührung
sie kränkte wie zu sehr Vertraulichkeit.

Sie war schon nicht mehr diese blonde Frau,
die in des Dichters Liedern manchmal anklang,
nicht mehr des breiten Bettes Duft und Eiland
und jenes Mannes Eigentum nicht mehr.

Sie war schon aufgelöst wie langes Haar
und hingegeben wie gefallner Regen
und ausgeteilt wie hundertfacher Vorrat.

Sie war schon Wurzel.

But now she walked at this god's hand,
her steps impeded by long winding-sheets,
unsure, slowly, without impatience.
She was within herself, great with expectation,
and gave no thought to the man going on ahead
or to the path leading up to life.
She was within herself. And her being dead
filled her like great plenitude.
Like a fruit, with its sweetness and darkness,
was she full with her great death,
so new to her she understood nothing.

She had come into another virginity
and wasn't to be touched; her sex was closed
like a young flower toward evening,
and her hands were by now so unused
to being wed that even the gentle god's
infinitely soft, light, guiding touch
offended her as too intimate.

She was no more the woman of flaxen hair
who sometimes resonated in the poet's songs,
no more the odor and island of the wide bed,
and that man's possession no more.

She was already loosened like long hair
and surrendered like fallen rain
and meted out like a hundred-fold supply.

Already she was root.

Und als plötzlich jäh
der Gott sie anhielt und mit Schmerz im Ausruf
die Worte sprach: Er hat sich umgewendet—,
begriff sie nichts und sagte leise: *Wer?*

Fern aber, dunkel vor dem klaren Ausgang,
stand irgend jemand, dessen Angesicht
nicht zu erkennen war. Er stand und sah,
wie auf dem Streifen eines Wiesenpfades
mit trauervollem Blick der Gott der Botschaft
sich schweigend wandte, der Gestalt zu folgen,
die schon zurückging dieses selben Weges,
den Schritt beschränkt von langen Leichenbändern,
unsicher, sanft und ohne Ungeduld.

And when suddenly, abruptly,
the god stopped her and in a pained voice
said: "He's turned around,"
she did not understand and quietly answered: "Who?"

In the distance, dark before the bright exit,
stood someone whose face
could not be recognized. He stood and saw
how on a strip of the meadow path
with mournful look the god of tidings
silently turned to follow the figure
who already had started back down,
her steps impeded by long winding-sheets,
unsure, slowly, without impatience.

DIE ROSENSCHALE

Zornige sahst du flackern, sahst zwei Knaben
zu einem Etwas sich zusammenballen,
das Haß war und sich auf der Erde wälzte
wie ein von Bienen überfallnes Tier;
Schauspieler, aufgetürmte Übertreiber,
rasende Pferde, die zusammenbrachen,
den Blick wegwerfend, bläkend das Gebiß
als schälte sich der Schädel aus dem Maule.

Nun aber weißt du, wie sich das vergißt:
denn vor dir steht die volle Rosenschale,
die unvergeßlich ist und angefüllt
mit jenem Äußersten von Sein und Neigen,
Hinhalten, Niemals-Gebenkönnen, Dastehn,
das unser sein mag: Äußerstes auch uns.

Lautloses Leben, Aufgehn ohne Ende,
Raum-brauchen ohne Raum von jenem Raum
zu nehmen, den die Dinge rings verringern,
fast nicht Umrissen-sein wie Ausgespartes
und lauter Inneres, viel seltsam Zartes
und Sich-bescheinendes—bis an den Rand:
ist irgend etwas uns bekannt wie dies?

Und dann wie dies: daß ein Gefühl entsteht,
weil Blütenblätter Blütenblätter rühren?
Und dies: daß eins sich aufschlägt wie ein Lid,
und drunter liegen lauter Augenlider,
geschlossene, als ob sie, zehnfach schlafend,

THE BOWL OF ROSES

You saw angry ones flare, saw two boys
clump themselves together into a something
that was pure hate, thrashing in the dirt
like an animal set upon by bees;
actors, piled-up exaggerators,
careening horses crashed to the ground,
their gaze discarded, baring their teeth
as if the skull peeled itself out through the mouth.

But now you know how these things are forgotten:
for here before you stands a full bowl of roses,
which is unforgettable and brimming
with ultimate instances of being and bowing down,
of offering, of being unable to give, of standing there
almost as part of us: ultimates for us too.

Noiseless living, opening without end,
filling space without taking space from the space
that all the other things in it diminish,
almost without an outline, like something omitted,
and pure inwardness, with much curious softness
shining into itself — right up to the rim:
is anything as known to us as this?

And this: that a feeling arises
because petals are being touched by petals?
And this: that one opens itself, like a lid,
and beneath lie many more eyelids,
all closed, as if, tenfold asleep, they

zu dämpfen hätten eines Innern Sehkraft.
Und dies vor allem: daß durch diese Blätter
das Licht hindurch muß. Aus den tausend Himmeln
filtern sie langsam jenen Tropfen Dunkel,
in dessen Feuerschein das wirre Bündel
der Staubgefäße sich erregt und aufbäumt.

Und die Bewegung in den Rosen, sieh:
Gebärden von so kleinem Ausschlagswinkel,
daß sie unsichtbar blieben, liefen ihre
Strahlen nicht auseinander in das Weltall.

Sieh jene weiße, die sich selig aufschlug
und dasteht in den großen offnen Blättern
wie eine Venus aufrecht in der Muschel;
und die errötende, die wie verwirrt
nach einer kühlen sich hinüberwendet,
und wie die kühle fühllos sich zurückzieht,
und wie die kalte steht, in sich gehüllt,
unter den offenen, die alles abtun.
Und *was* sie abtun, wie das leicht und schwer,
wie es ein Mantel, eine Last, ein Flügel
und eine Maske sein kann, je nach dem,
und *wie* sie's abtun: wie vor dem Geliebten.

Was können sie nicht sein: war jene gelbe,
die hohl und offen daliegt, nicht die Schale
von einer Frucht, darin dasselbe Gelb,
gesammelter, orangeröter, Saft war?
Und wars für diese schon zu viel, das Aufgehn,
weil an der Luft ihr namenloses Rosa
den bittern Nachgeschmack des Lila annahm?

must damp down an inner power to see.
And, above all, this: that through these petals
light has to pass. Slowly they filter out
from a thousand skies the drop of darkness
in whose fiery glow the jumbled bundle
of stamens becomes aroused and rears up.

And look, what activity in the roses:
gestures with angles of deflection so small
no one would notice them, were it not for
infinite space where their rays diverge.

See this white one, so blissfully opened,
standing among its huge spreading petals
like a Venus upright in her shell;
and look how that blushing one turns,
as if confused, toward the cooler one,
and how the cooler one, impassive, draws back,
and the cold one stands tightly wrapped in itself
among these opened ones, that shed everything.
And *what* they shed, how it can be
at once light and heavy, a cloak, a burden,
a wing, and a mask, it all depends,
and *how* they shed it: as before a lover.

Is there anything they *can't* be: wasn't this yellow one
that lies here hollow and open the rind
of a fruit of which the same yellow,
more intense, more orange-red, was the juice?
And this one, could opening have been too much for it,
since, touched by air, its indescribable pink
has picked up the bitter aftertaste of lilac?

Und die batistene, ist sie kein Kleid,
in dem noch zart und atemwarm das Hemd steckt,
mit dem zugleich es abgeworfen wurde
im Morgenschatten an dem alten Waldbad?
Und diese hier, opalnes Porzellan,
zerbrechlich, eine flache Chinatasse
und angefüllt mit kleinen hellen Faltern,—
und jene da, die nichts enthält als sich.

Und sind nicht alle so, nur sich enthaltend,
wenn Sich-enthalten heißt: die Welt da draußen
und Wind und Regen und Geduld des Frühlings
und Schuld und Unruh und vermummtes Schicksal
und Dunkelheit der abendlichen Erde
bis auf der Wolken Wandel, Flucht und Anflug,
bis auf den vagen Einfluß ferner Sterne
in eine Hand voll Innres zu verwandeln.

Nun liegt es sorglos in den offnen Rosen.

And isn't this batiste one a dress, with
the chemise still inside it, soft and breath-warm,
both garments flung off together
in morning shade at the bathing pool in the woods?
And this, opalescent porcelain,
fragile, a shallow china cup
filled with little lighted butterflies,—
and this, containing nothing but itself.

And aren't they all doing the same: simply containing them-
    selves,
if to contain oneself means: to transform the world outside
and wind and rain and patience of spring
and guilt and restlessness and disguised fate
and darkness of earth at evening
all the way to the errancy, flight, and coming on of clouds,
all the way to the vague influence of the distant stars
into a hand full of inwardness.

Now it lies free of cares in the open roses.

ARCHAÏSCHER TORSO APOLLOS

Wir kannten nicht sein unerhörtes Haupt,
darin die Augenäpfel reiften. Aber
sein Torso glüht noch wie ein Kandelaber,
in dem sein Schauen, nur zurückgeschraubt,

sich hält und glänzt. Sonst könnte nicht der Bug
der Brust dich blenden, und im leisen Drehen
der Lenden könnte nicht ein Lächeln gehen
zu jener Mitte, die die Zeugung trug.

Sonst stünde dieser Stein entstellt und kurz
unter der Schultern durchsichtigem Sturz
und flimmerte nicht so wie Raubtierfelle;

und bräche nicht aus allen seinen Rändern
aus wie ein Stern: denn da ist keine Stelle,
die dich nicht sieht. Du mußt dein Leben ändern.

ARCHAIC TORSO OF APOLLO

We never knew his stupendous head
in which the eye-apples ripened. But
his torso still glows, like a lamp,
in which his gaze, screwed back to low,

holds steady and gleams. Otherwise the curve
of his chest couldn't dazzle you, nor a smile
run through the slight twist of the loins
toward the center that held procreation.

Otherwise this stone would stand mutilated and too short
below the translucent fall-off of the shoulders,
and wouldn't shimmer like a predator's fur;

nor shine out past all its edges
like a star: for in it is no place
that doesn't see you. You must change your life.

LEDA

Als ihn der Gott in seiner Not betrat,
erschrak er fast, den Schwan so schön zu finden;
er ließ sich ganz verwirrt in ihm verschwinden.
Schon aber trug ihn sein Betrug zur Tat,

bevor er noch des unerprobten Seins
Gefühle prüfte. Und die Aufgetane
erkannte schon den Kommenden im Schwane
und wußte schon: er bat um Eins,

das sie, verwirrt in ihrem Widerstand,
nicht mehr verbergen konnte. Er kam nieder
und halsend durch die immer schwächre Hand

ließ sich der Gott in die Geliebte los.
Dann erst empfand er glücklich sein Gefieder
und wurde wirklich Schwan in ihrem Schoß.

LEDA

When the god in his need stepped across into him,
he was almost shocked to find the swan so beautiful;
and in his confusion he let himself disappear into him.
But the dissimulation swiftly led to the act,

before he could even test the feelings
of this untried state. And she, opened,
could already see who it was coming down in the swan
and knew at once: he asked for one thing,

which she, confused in her resistance,
no longer could hold back. He came down
and, pushing his neck through her weakening hand,

the god released himself into the beloved.
And then he took joy in his plumage
and really became a swan in her lap.

DON JUANS KINDHEIT

In seiner Schlankheit war, schon fast entscheidend,
der Bogen, der an Frauen nicht zerbricht;
und manchmal, seine Stirne nicht mehr meidend,
ging eine Neigung durch sein Angesicht

zu einer die vorüberkam, zu einer
die ihm ein fremdes altes Bild verschloß:
er lächelte. Er war nicht mehr der Weiner,
der sich ins Dunkel trug und sich vergoß.

Und während ein ganz neues Selbstvertrauen
ihn öfter tröstete und fast verzog,
ertrug er ernst den ganzen Blick der Frauen,
der ihn bewunderte und ihn bewog.

DON JUAN'S CHILDHOOD

In his slenderness, already almost the decisive factor,
was the bow that never failed him with women;
and sometimes, no longer avoiding being seen,
an inclination would rise into his face

towards a woman passing by, a woman
barred to him by a strange image from the past:
and he would smile. For he was no longer the weeper
who took himself off into the dark and shed himself.

And while this very new self-assurance
often soothed and nearly spoiled him,
he now could soberly bear the full gaze of women,
which admired him and moved him.

DIE FLAMINGOS

Jardin des Plantes, Paris

In Spiegelbildern wie von Fragonard
ist doch von ihrem Weiß und ihrer Röte
nicht mehr gegeben, als dir einer böte,
wenn er von seiner Freundin sagt: sie war

noch sanft von Schlaf. Denn steigen sie ins Grüne
und stehn, auf rosa Stielen leicht gedreht,
beisammen, blühend, wie in einem Beet,
verführen sie verführender als Phryne

sich selber, bis sie ihres Auges Bleiche
hinhalsend bergen in der eignen Weiche,
in welcher Schwarz und Fruchtrot sich versteckt.

Auf einmal kreischt ein Neid durch die Volière;
sie aber haben sich erstaunt gestreckt
und schreiten einzeln ins Imaginäre.

THE FLAMINGOS
Jardin des Plantes, Paris

In these Fragonard-like mirrorings
no more of their white and pink
is proffered than if a man
said of his mistress: "So soft

she was with sleep." Then, stepping up into the grass,
and standing, slightly turned, on pink stems,
blossoming together as in a flowerbed,
they seduce themselves more seductively than Phryne did,

herself; and then, extending their necks,
they burrow their eyes' paleness into their own softness,
in which black and fruit-red lies hidden.

Immediately shrieks of jealousy go through the aviary;
but already, astonished, they have stretched themselves
and stride off one by one into the imaginary.

from REQUIEM

REQUIEM FÜR EINE FREUNDIN

Ich habe Tote, und ich ließ sie hin
und war erstaunt, sie so getrost zu sehn,
so rasch zuhaus im Totsein, so gerecht,
so anders als ihr Ruf. Nur du, du kehrst
zurück; du streifst mich, du gehst um, du willst
an etwas stoßen, daß es klingt von dir
und dich verrät. O nimm mir nicht, was ich
langsam erlern. Ich habe recht; du irrst
wenn du gerührt zu irgend einem Ding
ein Heimweh hast. Wir wandeln dieses um;
es ist nicht hier, wir spiegeln es herein
aus unserm Sein, sobald wir es erkennen.

   Ich glaubte dich viel weiter. Mich verwirrts,
daß *du* gerade irrst und kommst, die mehr
verwandelt hat als irgend eine Frau.
Daß wir erschraken, da du starbst, nein, daß
dein starker Tod uns dunkel unterbrach,
das Bisdahin abreißend vom Seither:
das geht uns an; das einzuordnen wird
die Arbeit sein, die wir mit allem tun.
Doch daß du selbst erschrakst und auch noch jetzt
den Schrecken hast, wo Schrecken nicht mehr gilt;
daß du von deiner Ewigkeit ein Stück
verlierst und hier hereintrittst, Freundin, hier,
wo alles noch nicht *ist*; daß du zerstreut,
zum ersten Mal im All zerstreut und halb,
den Aufgang der unendlichen Naturen
nicht so ergriffst wie hier ein jedes Ding;
daß aus dem Kreislauf, der dich schon empfing,
die stumme Schwerkraft irgend einer Unruh

REQUIEM FOR A FRIEND

I have my dead and I have let them go
and been surprised, to see them so consoled,
so soon at home in death, just right this way,
so unlike what we hear. Only you, you come
back; you brush against me, you move about, you want
to knock into things, to make them sound of you
and tell me you're here. Oh don't take away what
I'm slowly learning. For I'm right; you're mistaken
if, looking back, you feel homesickness
for any thing here. We transform it;
it isn't here, we mirror it into us,
out of existence, the moment we can see it.

   I thought you'd be further along. It bewilders me
that you of all people err and come back, you,
who did more transforming than any other woman.
That your death frightened us, or, no, that
your hard death darkly broke in upon us
and tore what went before from what came after:
this is a matter for us; sorting it out
now will be our task in everything we do.
But that you were frightened yourself and even now
feel terror, where terror doesn't apply;
that you could give up a portion of your
eternity, and enter here, dear friend, here,
where everything not yet *is*; that, distracted in endless space,
for the first time, distracted and incomplete, you
couldn't grasp the dawning of eternal natures
the way, here, you grasped each smallest thing;
and that, from the circulation that has already received you,
the mute gravity of some disquiet

dich niederzieht zur abgezählten Zeit—:
dies weckt mich nachts oft wie ein Dieb, der einbricht.
Und dürft ich sagen, daß du nur geruhst,
daß du aus Großmut kommst, aus Überfülle,
weil du so sicher bist, so in dir selbst,
daß du herumgehst wie ein Kind, nicht bange
vor Örtern, wo man einem etwas tut—:
doch nein: du bittest. Dieses geht mir so
bis ins Gebein und querrt wie eine Säge.
Ein Vorwurf, den du trügest als Gespenst,
nachtrügest mir, wenn ich mich nachts zurückzieh
in meine Lunge, in die Eingeweide,
in meines Herzens letzte ärmste Kammer,—
ein solcher Vorwurf wäre nicht so grausam,
wie dieses Bitten ist. Was bittest du?

　　Sag, soll ich reisen? Hast du irgendwo
ein Ding zurückgelassen, das sich quält
und das dir nachwill? Soll ich in ein Land,
das du nicht sahst, obwohl es dir verwandt
war wie die andre Hälfte deiner Sinne?

　　Ich will auf seinen Flüssen fahren, will
an Land gehn und nach alten Sitten fragen,
will mit den Frauen in den Türen sprechen
und zusehn, wenn sie ihre Kinder rufen.
Ich will mir merken, wie sie dort die Landschaft
umnehmen draußen bei der alten Arbeit
der Wiesen und der Felder; will begehren,
vor ihren König hingeführt zu sein,
und will die Priester durch Bestechung reizen,
daß sie mich legen vor das stärkste Standbild
und fortgehn und die Tempeltore schließen.
Dann aber will ich, wenn ich vieles weiß,

drags you back into counted time—:
all this often wakes me at night like a thief breaking in.
If only I could say: that you deign,
deign to come back, out of magnanimity and overabundance,
so secure in yourself, so self-contained
that you can wander freely, like a child, unafraid
of the places where someone could do you harm—:
but no: you're pleading. This cuts
to the bone and rauks like a saw.
Whatever rebuke that you, as ghost, could
bear against me in the night, when I retract
into my lungs, into my guts,
into the last, poorest chamber of my heart,—
could never be so gruesome
as this pleading. What are you pleading for?

    Tell me, do you want me to travel? Did you
leave some thing behind somewhere, a thing now in torment,
that wants to follow you? Should I look in a country
you never saw, though it was as kindred
to you as the other half of your senses?

    I'll take passage up its rivers,
go ashore and inquire about its old customs,
speak with the women in their doorways
and observe as they call to their children.
I'll watch how they wrap themselves in the land
while at their ancient labor
in the meadows and fields; I'll insist
on being brought before the king,
and slip money to the priests to take me
and lay me down before their most powerful idol
and leave, closing the temple gates.
Then, when I've learned enough, I'll

einfach die Tiere anschaun, daß ein Etwas
von ihrer Wendung mir in die Gelenke
herübergleitet; will ein kurzes Dasein
in ihren Augen haben, die mich halten
und langsam lassen, ruhig, ohne Urteil.
Ich will mir von den Gärtnern viele Blumen
hersagen lassen, daß ich in den Scherben
der schönen Eigennamen einen Rest
herüberbringe von den hundert Düften.
Und Früchte will ich kaufen, Früchte, drin
das Land noch einmal ist, bis an den Himmel.

Denn Das verstandest du: die vollen Früchte.
Die legtest du auf Schalen vor dich hin
und wogst mit Farben ihre Schwere auf.
Und so wie Früchte sahst du auch die Fraun
und sahst die Kinder so, von innen her
getrieben in die Formen ihres Daseins.
Und sahst dich selbst zuletzt wie eine Frucht,
nahmst dich heraus aus deinen Kleidern, trugst
dich vor den Spiegel, ließest dich hinein
bis auf dein Schauen; das blieb groß davor
und sagte nicht: das bin ich; nein: dies ist.
So ohne Neugier war zuletzt dein Schaun
und so besitzlos, von so wahrer Armut,
daß es dich selbst nicht mehr begehrte: heilig.

So will ich dich behalten, wie du dich
hinstelltest in den Spiegel, tief hinein
und fort von allem. Warum kommst du anders?
Was widerrufst du dich? Was willst du mir
einreden, daß in jenen Bernsteinkugeln
um deinen Hals noch etwas Schwere war

simply watch the animals, letting something
in how they move glide over into my
joints; and I'll have a brief existence
in their eyes, which hold me
and then let me go, slowly, peacefully, without judging.
I'll ask the gardeners what they call
the many flowers, so that in the small crocks
of their lovely proper names I can bring back
remnants of the hundred fragrances.
And fruit, yes, I'll buy fruit, fruit in which
the country exists once again, right up to its sky.

   For these are things you understood: full fruit.
You set them out in bowls before you,
weighing their heaviness with your colors.
In the same way as you saw fruit, you saw women,
and children, too, driven from within
into the forms of their existence.
And finally you saw even yourself as a fruit,
and took yourself out of your clothes and carried
yourself before the mirror and let yourself go in,
all in, but for your gaze; great, it stayed outside,
and didn't say: "That's me"; but: "This is."
And at last your looking was so incurious,
so free of possessing, and of such true poverty
that it no longer desired even you yourself: holy.

   This is how I would keep you, seeing you placing
yourself before the mirror, deep inside it
far from everything. Why come back this way?
Why change things now? Would you talk me into
believing that in those amber beads
at your neck was something even heavier

von jener Schwere, wie sie nie im Jenseits
beruhigter Bilder ist; was zeigst du mir
in deiner Haltung eine böse Ahnung;
was heißt dich die Konturen deines Leibes
auslegen wie die Linien einer Hand,
daß ich sie nicht mehr sehn kann ohne Schicksal?

Komm her ins Kerzenlicht. Ich bin nicht bang,
die Toten anzuschauen. Wenn sie kommen,
so haben sie ein Recht, in unserm Blick
sich aufzuhalten, wie die andern Dinge.

Komm her; wir wollen eine Weile still sein.
Sieh diese Rose an auf meinem Schreibtisch;
ist nicht das Licht um sie genau so zaghaft
wie über dir: sie dürfte auch nicht hier sein.
Im Garten draußen, unvermischt mit mir,
hätte sie bleiben müssen oder hingehn,—
nun währt sie so: was ist ihr mein Bewußtsein?

Erschrick nicht, wenn ich jetzt begreife, ach,
da steigt es in mir auf: ich kann nicht anders,
ich muß begreifen, und wenn ich dran stürbe.
Begreifen, daß du hier bist. Ich begreife.
Ganz wie ein Blinder rings ein Ding begreift,
fühl ich dein Los und weiß ihm keinen Namen.
Laß uns zusammen klagen, daß dich einer
aus deinem Spiegel nahm. Kannst du noch weinen?
Du kannst nicht. Deiner Tränen Kraft und Andrang
hast du verwandelt in dein reifes Anschaun
und warst dabei, jeglichen Saft in dir
so umzusetzen in ein starkes Dasein,
das steigt und kreist, im Gleichgewicht und blindlings.

than the heaviness that is never in the heaven
of peaceful pictures; why must you let me see
the ill omen in how you hold yourself;
and what could lead you to construe your body's
contours as lines in the palm of a hand,
so that now I can't see them apart from fate?

    Come here into the candlelight. I'm not afraid to
look at the dead. For when the dead come
they have as much right to sojourn
in our gaze as any other thing.

    Come here; let's be silent for a bit.
Look at the rose on my desk;
isn't the light around it as hesitant
as the light shining above you: it shouldn't be here either.
Out in the garden, uninvolved with me,
it should have kept on living or died,
now it's just lasting it out: what's my consciousness to it, anyway?

    Don't be afraid if I grasp it now, ah,
now it rises in me: I can't help myself,
I must grasp it, even if I die of it.
Grasp that you're here. And I do grasp it.
As a blind person grasps some nearby thing,
I feel your lot yet can't name it.
Let's lament together that someone
could take you out of your mirror. Can you still cry?
You can't. You transformed the force and urgency
of your tears into your mature gaze
and were just on the point of turning all your
body's juices into a powerful existence,
which would rise and circle, trustingly, in equilibrium.

Da riß ein Zufall dich, dein letzter Zufall
riß dich zurück aus deinem fernsten Fortschritt
in eine Welt zurück, wo Säfte *wollen*.
Riß dich nicht ganz; riß nur ein Stück zuerst,
doch als um dieses Stück von Tag zu Tag
die Wirklichkeit so zunahm, daß es schwer ward,
da brauchtest du dich ganz: da gingst du hin
und brachst in Brocken dich aus dem Gesetz
mühsam heraus, weil du dich brauchtest. Da
trugst du dich ab und grubst aus deines Herzens
nachtwarmem Erdreich die noch grünen Samen,
daraus dein Tod aufkeimen sollte: deiner,
dein eigner Tod zu deinem eignen Leben.
Und aßest sie, die Körner deines Todes,
wie alle andern, aßest seine Körner,
und hattest Nachgeschmack in dir von Süße,
die du nicht meintest, hattest süße Lippen,
du: die schon innen in den Sinnen süß war.

    O laß uns klagen. Weißt du, wie dein Blut
aus einem Kreisen ohnegleichen zögernd
und ungern wiederkam, da du es abriefst?
Wie es verwirrt des Leibes kleinen Kreislauf
noch einmal aufnahm; wie es voller Mißtraun
und Staunen eintrat in den Mutterkuchen
und von dem weiten Rückweg plötzlich müd war.
Du triebst es an, du stießest es nach vorn,
du zerrtest es zur Feuerstelle, wie
man eine Herde Tiere zerrt zum Opfer;
und wolltest noch, es sollte dabei froh sein.
Und du erzwangst es schließlich: es war froh
und lief herbei und gab sich hin. Dir schien,
weil du gewohnt warst an die andern Maße,

Then chance, your last encounter with chance,
tore you back from your furthest progress,
back into a world where juices have their will.
Not all at once; tore just a shred at first,
but when, around this shred, day by day,
reality swelled, became heavy,
then you needed all of yourself: then you went
and broke yourself into pieces, laboriously freeing
yourself from the law, because you needed yourself. Then
you cleared the debris and dug from your heart's
night-warm soil the still-green seeds
from which your death was to germinate: your own death,
the death that was yours during your own life.
And ate them, ate these kernels of your death,
as you had all the others, ate the kernels
that left in you an aftertaste of sweetness
you hadn't expected, and gave you sweet lips,
you: who within your senses were already sweet.

    Yes, let's lament. Do you know how haltingly,
how begrudgingly, your blood turned back,
when you summoned it from its incomparable circling?
And how bewildered it was to take up again
the body's trivial circulations; and with what mistrust
and astonishment it entered the placenta,
and then suddenly it was tired from the long journey back.
And you drove it, you shoved it forward,
you dragged it to the site of fire, as
one flails a group of animals to the sacrifice;
and you even wanted it to be happy there.
And at last you compelled it: and it was happy,
and it ran to you and surrendered itself up. You thought,
because you were used to another scale,

es wäre nur für eine Weile; aber
nun warst du in der Zeit, und Zeit ist lang.
Und Zeit geht hin, und Zeit nimmt zu, und Zeit
ist wie ein Rückfall einer langen Krankheit.

Wie war dein Leben kurz, wenn du's vergleichst
mit jenen Stunden, da du saßest und
die vielen Kräfte deiner vielen Zukunft
schweigend herabbogst zu dem neuen Kindkeim,
der wieder Schicksal war. O wehe Arbeit.
O Arbeit über alle Kraft. Du tatest
sie Tag für Tag, du schlepptest dich zu ihr
und zogst den schönen Einschlag aus dem Webstuhl
und brauchtest alle deine Fäden anders.
Und endlich hattest du noch Mut zum Fest.

Denn da's getan war, wolltest du belohnt sein,
wie Kinder, wenn sie bittersüßen Tee
getrunken haben, der vielleicht gesund macht.
So lohntest du dich: denn von jedem andern
warst du zu weit, auch jetzt noch; keiner hätte
ausdenken können, welcher Lohn dir wohltut.
Du wußtest es. Du saßest auf im Kindbett,
und vor dir stand ein Spiegel, der dir alles
ganz wiedergab. Nun war das alles *Du*
und ganz *davor*, und drinnen war nur Täuschung,
die schöne Täuschung jeder Frau, die gern
Schmuck umnimmt und das Haar kämmt und verändert.

So starbst du, wie die Frauen früher starben,
altmodisch starbst du in dem warmen Hause
den Tod der Wöchnerinnen, welche wieder
sich schließen wollen und es nicht mehr können,
weil jenes Dunkel, das sie mitgebaren,
noch einmal wiederkommt und drängt und eintritt.

that it would take but a little while; but
now you were in time, and time is long.
And time passes, and time increases, and time
is like a relapse into an endless illness.

How short your life turned out to be, measured
against those hours when you sat silently
bending the many energies of your multifarious
future back down into this new child-sprout,
which once again was fate. O painful labor.
O labor beyond all strength. Day after day
you did it, dragged yourself to it,
extracted the lovely weft from the loom
and used all your threads in another way.
And in the end you still had the spirit to celebrate.

Once it was done, you wanted your reward,
as children do when they've drunk down
the bittersweet infusion that might make them well.
Here's how you rewarded yourself: for even then you were
so far ahead of all the others; no one
could have imagined the reward that would have pleased you.
But you knew. You sat up in the birthing-bed,
and before you stood a mirror that gave you back
yourself whole. Now all that was *you*,
all that *in front*; and inside was only deception,
the lovely deception of every woman who likes
to spread out her jewelry, who combs her hair and changes.

And so you died, the way women used to die,
died in that warm house the old-fashioned
death of women in childbed, who wanted to close
themselves again, and no longer could,
because the darkness they'd also given birth to
comes back and insists and enters.

Ob man nicht dennoch hätte Klagefrauen
auftreiben müssen? Weiber, welche weinen
für Geld, und die man so bezahlen kann,
daß sie die Nacht durch heulen, wenn es still wird.
Gebräuche her! wir haben nicht genug
Gebräuche. Alles geht und wird verredet.
So mußt du kommen, tot, und hier mit mir
Klagen nachholen. Hörst du, daß ich klage?
Ich möchte meine Stimme wie ein Tuch
hinwerfen über deines Todes Scherben
und zerrn an ihr, bis sie in Fetzen geht,
und alles, was ich sage, müßte so
zerlumpt in dieser Stimme gehn und frieren;
blieb es beim Klagen. Doch jetzt klag ich an:
den Einen nicht, der dich aus dir zurückzog,
(ich find ihn nicht heraus, er ist wie alle)
doch alle klag ich in ihm an: den Mann.

Wenn irgendwo ein Kindgewesensein
tief in mir aufsteigt, das ich noch nicht kenne,
vielleicht das reinste Kindsein meiner Kindheit:
ich wills nicht wissen. Einen Engel will
ich daraus bilden ohne hinzusehn
und will ihn werfen in die erste Reihe
schreiender Engel, welche Gott erinnern.

Denn dieses Leiden dauert schon zu lang,
und keiner kanns; es ist zu schwer für uns,
das wirre Leiden von der falschen Liebe,
die, bauend auf Verjährung wie Gewohnheit,
ein Recht sich nennt und wuchert aus dem Unrecht.
Wo ist ein Mann, der Recht hat auf Besitz?

Perhaps, after all, we should have rounded up
some wailing women? Women who weep
out loud for money, whom one can pay
to bawl all through the quiet hours of the night.
Oh, how we need customs. Oh, how we suffer from the lack
of customs. They pass, we talk them out of existence.
And this is why you had to come back, yourself, dead, and help
here with me catch up on all the lamenting. Can you hear
        me wail?
I would swirl out my voice like a wide cloth
to cover the shards of your death
and then rend it until it was torn to shreds,
and everything I'd say from then on would
wear, shivering, the tatters of this voice;
if lament were enough. But now also I indict:
not him who wrenched you back out of yourself,
(I can't find him, he's like all the others)
but, in him, I accuse them all: all men.

    If somewhere deep within me arises some essence
of having been a child, one I never experienced,
perhaps the purest childness of my childhood,
I don't want to know it. Without even looking,
I want to form an angel out of it
and hurl him into the foremost rank
of screaming angels, to remind God.

    For this suffering has gone on too long,
none of us can bear it; it's too heavy,
this tangled suffering caused by false love, which,
relying on antiquated conventions as well as habit,
claims the right to extort riches from a wrong.
What man has the right to own?

Wer kann besitzen, was sich selbst nicht hält,
was sich von Zeit zu Zeit nur selig auffängt
und wieder hinwirft wie ein Kind den Ball.
Sowenig wie der Feldherr eine Nike
festhalten kann am Vorderbug des Schiffes,
wenn das geheime Leichtsein ihrer Gottheit
sie plötzlich weghebt in den hellen Meerwind:
so wenig kann einer von uns die Frau
anrufen, die uns nicht mehr sieht und die
auf einem schmalen Streifen ihres Daseins
wie durch ein Wunder fortgeht, ohne Unfall:
er hätte denn Beruf und Lust zur Schuld.

  Denn *das* ist Schuld, wenn irgendeines Schuld ist:
die Freiheit eines Lieben nicht vermehren
um alle Freiheit, die man in sich aufbringt.
Wir haben, wo wir lieben, ja nur dies:
einander lassen; denn daß wir uns halten,
das fällt uns leicht und ist nicht erst zu lernen.

  Bist du noch da? In welcher Ecke bist du?—
Du hast so viel gewußt von alledem
und hast so viel gekonnt, da du so hingingst
für alles offen, wie ein Tag, der anbricht.
Die Frauen leiden: lieben heißt allein sein,
und Künstler ahnen manchmal in der Arbeit,
daß sie verwandeln müssen, wo sie lieben.
Beides begannst du; beides ist in Dem,
was jetzt ein Ruhm entstellt, der es dir fortnimmt.
Ach du warst weit von jedem Ruhm. Du warst
unscheinbar; hattest leise deine Schönheit
hineingenommen, wie man eine Fahne
einzieht am grauen Morgen eines Werktags,

Or to possess what can't hold on to itself,
but every so often blissfully catches itself
and tosses itself out again, as a child with a ball.
As little can the captain possess
a Nike at the bowsprit of his ship
when the secret lightness of her godhead
suddenly lifts her high into the bright sea wind:
so little can any man call back
the woman who no longer sees us, and who,
along a narrow isthmus of existence,
miraculously walks off unharmed,
unless his profession and pleasure be guilt.

    For this is guilt, if it is anything:
to fail to increase the freedom of a love
by all the freedom we can raise within ourselves.
When we love, we have, at most, this:
to let each other go; for holding on
comes easily, we don't have to learn it.

    Are you still here? In which corner are you?—
You knew so much about all these things,
and were so able, as you proceeded through life,
open to everything, like a dawning day.
Women suffer: to love means being alone,
and artists sometimes intuit in their work
that when they love, they must transform.
You began both tasks; we see it in everything
that fame now distorts and takes from you.
Ah, you were far beyond any fame. You were
inconspicuous, and quietly gathered
your beauty into yourself, as one takes in
a flag on a gray workday morning,

und wolltest nichts, als eine lange Arbeit,——
die nicht getan ist: dennoch nicht getan.

Wenn du noch da bist, wenn in diesem Dunkel
noch eine Stelle ist, an der dein Geist
empfindlich mitschwingt auf den flachen Schallwelln,
die eine Stimme, einsam in der Nacht,
aufregt in eines hohen Zimmers Strömung:
So hör mich: Hilf mir. Sieh, wir gleiten so,
nicht wissend wann, zurück aus unserm Fortschritt
in irgendwas, was wir nicht meinen; drin
wir uns verfangen wie in einem Traum
und drin wir sterben, ohne zu erwachen.
Keiner ist weiter. Jedem, der sein Blut
hinaufhob in ein Werk, das lange wird,
kann es geschehen, daß ers nicht mehr hochhält
und daß es geht nach seiner Schwere, wertlos.
Denn irgendwo ist eine alte Feindschaft
zwischen dem Leben und der großen Arbeit.
Daß ich sie einseh und sie sage: hilf mir.

Komm nicht zurück. Wenn du's erträgst, so sei
tot bei den Toten. Tote sind beschäftigt.
Doch hilf mir so, daß es dich nicht zerstreut,
wie mir das Fernste manchmal hilft: in mir.

and wanted nothing but a long-term work,—
which remains undone: ever undone.

    If you're still nearby, if somewhere in this darkness
there's a place where your spirit
resonates with the shallow sound-waves
a solitary voice can stir at night
in the currents of a high-ceilinged room:
Then hear me: Help me. You see, we slip back,
without knowing it, from our advance,
into something we didn't intend; where
we can become caught up, as in a dream,
and where we could die without waking.
No one went further. It can happen to any of us
who raise our blood to an extended work,
that we can't hold it at that level,
and it falls of its own weight, worthless.
For somewhere an old enmity exists
between our life and the great works we do.
So that I may have insight into it and say it: help me.

    Don't come back. If you can bear it, stay
dead among the dead. The dead have their tasks.
Then help me in a way that won't distract you,
as what is farthest sometimes helps me: within me.

from THE LIFE OF MARY

STILLUNG MARIAE MIT DEM AUFERSTANDENEN

Was sie damals empfanden: ist es nicht
vor allen Geheimnissen süß
und immer noch irdisch:
da er, ein wenig blaß noch vom Grab,
erleichtert zu ihr trat:
an allen Stellen erstanden.
O zu ihr zuerst. Wie waren sie da
unaussprechlich in Heilung.
Ja sie heilten, das war's. Sie hatten nicht nötig,
sich stark zu berühren.
Er legte ihr eine Sekunde
kaum seine nächstens
ewige Hand an die frauliche Schulter.
Und sie begannen
still wie die Bäume im Frühling,
unendlich zugleich,
diese Jahreszeit
ihres äußersten Umgangs.

THE QUIETING OF MARY WITH
THE RESURRECTED ONE

What they felt then: is it not
above all other mysteries the sweetest
and yet still earthly:
when he, pale from the grave,
his burdens laid down, went to her:
risen in all places.
Oh, first to her. How they
inexpressibly began to heal.
Yes, to heal: that simple. They felt no need
to touch each other strongly.
He placed his hand, which next
would be eternal, for scarcely
a second on her womanly shoulder.
And they began
quietly as trees in spring
in infinite simultaneity
their season
of ultimate communing.

UNCOLLECTED

[Lange mußt du leiden]

Lange mußt du leiden, kennend nicht was,
bis plötzlich aus gehässig erbissener Frucht
deines Leidens Geschmack eintritt in dir.
Und da liebst du schon fast das Gekostete. Keiner
redet dirs wieder aus

[Long you must suffer]

Long you must suffer, not knowing what,
until suddenly, from a piece of fruit hatefully bitten,
the taste of the suffering enters you.
And then you already almost love what you've savored. No one
will talk it out of you again.

DER TOD

Da steht der Tod, ein bläulicher Absud
in einer Tasse ohne Untersatz.
Ein wunderlicher Platz für eine Tasse:
steht auf dem Rücken einer Hand. Ganz gut
erkennt man noch an dem glasierten Schwung
den Bruch des Henkels. Staubig. Und: *"Hoff-nung"*
an ihrem Bug in aufgebrauchter Schrift.

Das hat der Trinker, den der Trank betrifft,
bei einem fernen Frühstück ab-gelesen.

Was sind denn das für Wesen,
die man zuletzt wegschrecken muß mit Gift?

Blieben sie sonst? Sind sie denn hier vernarrt
in dieses Essen voller Hindernis?
Man muß ihnen die harte Gegenwart
ausnehmen, wie ein künstliches Gebiß.
Dann lallen sie.   Gelall, Gelall . . . .
. . . .

O Sternenfall,
von einer Brücke einmal eingesehn—:
Dich nicht vergessen. Stehn!

DEATH

There death stands, a bluish residue
in a cup without a saucer.
Odd place for a cup:
standing on the back of a hand. It's easy
to make out where the handle broke off
on the glazed roundness. Dusty. With: *"Hope"*
on its curve in lettering all but worn off.

The person the drink was intended for
read it off at some long-ago breakfast.

What kind of beings are these anyway,
who in the end have to be scared away with poison?

Would they never leave, otherwise? Can they be that besotted
by this meal full of obstacles?
The hard present has to be taken out
of them like a set of false teeth.
Then they start slurring. Mumble, mumble . . . .
. . . .

O falling star
seen once from a bridge—:
Never to forget you. Stay standing!

[Von meiner Antwort weiß ich noch nicht]

Von meiner Antwort weiß ich noch nicht
wann ich sie sagen werde.
Aber, horch eine Harke, die schon schafft.
Oben allein im Weinberg spricht
schon ein Mann mit der Erde.

[I'm not sure yet when]

I'm not sure yet when
you'll have my response.
But, listen: a rake at work this early.
Above, alone, in the vineyard, a man
is already talking with the earth.

[An der sonngewohnten Straße]

An der sonngewohnten Straße, in dem
hohlen halben Baumstamm, der seit lange
Trog ward, eine Oberfläche Wasser
in sich leis erneuernd, still' ich meinen
Durst: des Wassers Heiterkeit und Herkunft
in mich nehmend durch die Handgelenke.
Trinken schiene mir zu viel, zu deutlich;
aber diese wartende Gebärde
holt mir helles Wasser ins Bewußtsein.

Also, kämst du, braucht ich, mich zu stillen,
nur ein leichtes Anruhn meiner Hände,
sei's an deiner Schulter junge Rundung,
sei es an den Andrang deiner Brüste.

[At the road used to sun]

At the road used to sun, in the
halved hollow log long ago become
a drinking trough, a surface of water
renewing itself silently from within, I still
my thirst, drawing in through my wrists
the clarity and origin of the water.
To drink would seem to me too much, too overt,
but this long-lingering gesture
lifts bright water into consciousness.

Just so, if you came, all I would need to quieten me
would be a light resting of my hands,
be it on the youthful roundness of your shoulders,
be it on the urging pressure of your breasts.

DUINO ELEGIES

DIE ERSTE ELEGIE

Wer, wenn ich schriee, hörte mich denn aus der Engel
Ordnungen? und gesetzt selbst, es nähme
einer mich plötzlich ans Herz: ich verginge von seinem
stärkeren Dasein. Denn das Schöne ist nichts
als des Schrecklichen Anfang, den wir noch grade ertragen,
und wir bewundern es so, weil es gelassen verschmäht,
uns zu zerstören. Ein jeder Engel ist schrecklich.
    Und so verhalt ich mich denn und verschlucke den Lockruf
dunkelen Schluchzens. Ach, wen vermögen
wir denn zu brauchen? Engel nicht, Menschen nicht,
und die findigen Tiere merken es schon,
daß wir nicht sehr verläßlich zu Haus sind
in der gedeuteten Welt. Es bleibt uns vielleicht
irgend ein Baum an dem Abhang, daß wir ihn täglich
wiedersähen; es bleibt uns die Straße von gestern
und das verzogene Treusein einer Gewohnheit,
der es bei uns gefiel, und so blieb sie und ging nicht.
    O und die Nacht, die Nacht, wenn der Wind voller
        Weltraum
uns am Angesicht zehrt—, wem bliebe sie nicht, die ersehnte,
sanft enttäuschende, welche dem einzelnen Herzen
mühsam bevorsteht. Ist sie den Liebenden leichter?
Ach, sie verdecken sich nur mit einander ihr Los.
    Weißt du's *noch* nicht? Wirf aus den Armen die Leere
zu den Räumen hinzu, die wir atmen; vielleicht daß die Vögel
die erweiterte Luft fühlen mit innigerm Flug.

THE FIRST ELEGY

Who, if I screamed out, would hear among the hierarchies
of angels? And if one suddenly did take
me to his heart: I would perish from his
stronger existence. For beauty is nothing
but the onset of terror we're still just able to bear,
and we admire it so because it calmly disdains
to destroy us. Every angel is terrifying.
    And so I hold back and swallow the lure-call
of dark sobbing. Ah, who can we prevail upon
to use in our need? Not angels, not humans,
and the insightful animals already note
we're not very securely at home
in the interpreted world. Maybe there remains for us
a tree, seen on its hillslope every day
as we pass; and yesterday's street
and the indulgent loyalty of a habit
that liked being with us and settled in and never left.
    Oh, and the night, the night, when wind full of cosmic space
feasts on our faces—, for whom would she not remain, that
    yearned-for
tenderly undeceiving one, who awaits with such travail
each solitary heart. Is it easier for lovers?
Oh, they use each other to hide themselves from their fate.
    Don't you know that *yet*? Fling the emptiness out of your
    arms
into the spaces we breathe; so that in the expanded air
birds might feel themselves more inwardly flying.

Ja, die Frühlinge brauchten dich wohl. Es muteten manche
Sterne dir zu, daß du sie spürtest. Es hob
sich eine Woge heran im Vergangenen, oder
da du vorüberkamst am geöffneten Fenster,
gab eine Geige sich hin. Das alles war Auftrag.
Aber bewältigtest du's? Warst du nicht immer
noch von Erwartung zerstreut, als kündigte alles
eine Geliebte dir an? (Wo willst du sie bergen,
da doch die großen fremden Gedanken bei dir
aus und ein gehn und öfters bleiben bei Nacht.)
Sehnt es dich aber, so singe die Liebenden; lange
noch nicht unsterblich genug ist ihr berühmtes Gefühl.
Jene, du neidest sie fast, Verlassenen, die du
so viel liebender fandst als die Gestillten. Beginn
immer von neuem die nie zu erreichende Preisung;
denk: es erhält sich der Held, selbst der Untergang war ihm
nur ein Vorwand, zu sein: seine letzte Geburt.
Aber die Liebenden nimmt die erschöpfte Natur
in sich zurück, als wären nicht zweimal die Kräfte,
dieses zu leisten. Hast du der Gaspara Stampa
denn genügend gedacht, daß irgend ein Mädchen,
dem der Geliebte entging, am gesteigerten Beispiel
dieser Liebenden fühlt: daß ich würde wie sie?
Sollen nicht endlich uns diese ältesten Schmerzen
fruchtbarer werden? Ist es nicht Zeit, daß wir liebend
uns vom Geliebten befrein und es bebend bestehn:
wie der Pfeil die Sehne besteht, um gesammelt im Absprung
mehr zu sein als er selbst. Denn Bleiben ist nirgends.

Yes, the springtimes needed you. There were stars
counting on you to sense them. A wave
rose toward you in the past, or
when you walked under an opened window
a violin gave itself up to you. All this was commission.
Were you up to it? Weren't you always
distracted by expectation, as if all these announced
the arrival of a beloved? (Where will you tuck her away,
with all those great strange thoughts going in and out
and often even spending the night.)
No, when longing fills you, sing of the lovers;
their famed emotion isn't nearly immortal enough.
The forsaken ones, whom you almost envy, whom you've
found so much more loving than the requited. Begin
each time anew the praising that is never enough;
remember: heroes live on, even their downfall was
only a way of attaining: their final birth.
But lovers, nature, exhausted, gathers
back into itself, as if lacking the doubled strength
to do this for them. Have you memorialized
Gaspara Stampa so fully, that now any woman
whose beloved has eluded her might feel, thanks to this lover's
heightened example: "If only I could be like her?
Couldn't this oldest of sufferings finally be for us
more fruitful? Isn't it time that lovingly
we freed ourselves from our lover and, trembling, endured it:
as the arrow endures the bowstring, to be collected in its
        leap-off
into more than itself? For staying put is nowhere."

Stimmen, Stimmen. Höre, mein Herz, wie sonst nur
Heilige hörten: daß sie der riesige Ruf
aufhob vom Boden; sie aber knieten,
Unmögliche, weiter und achtetens nicht:
So waren sie hörend. Nicht, daß du *Gottes* ertrügest
die Stimme, bei weitem. Aber das Wehende höre,
die ununterbrochene Nachricht, die aus Stille sich bildet.
Es rauscht jetzt von jenen jungen Toten zu dir.
Wo immer du eintratst, redete nicht in Kirchen
zu Rom und Neapel ruhig ihr Schicksal dich an?
Oder es trug eine Inschrift sich erhaben dir auf,
wie neulich die Tafel in Santa Maria Formosa.
Was sie mir wollen? leise soll ich des Unrechts
Anschein abtun, der ihrer Geister
reine Bewegung manchmal ein wenig behindert.

Freilich ist es seltsam, die Erde nicht mehr zu bewohnen,
kaum erlernte Gebräuche nicht mehr zu üben,
Rosen, und andern eigens versprechenden Dingen
nicht die Bedeutung menschlicher Zukunft zu geben;
das, was man war in unendlich ängstlichen Händen,
nicht mehr zu sein, und selbst den eigenen Namen
wegzulassen wie ein zerbrochenes Spielzeug.
Seltsam, die Wünsche nicht weiterzuwünschen. Seltsam,
alles, was sich bezog, so lose im Raume
flattern zu sehen. Und das Totsein ist mühsam
und voller Nachholn, daß man allmählich ein wenig
Ewigkeit spürt.—Aber Lebendige machen
alle den Fehler, daß sie zu stark unterscheiden.
Engel (sagt man) wüßten oft nicht, ob sie unter
Lebenden gehn oder Toten. Die ewige Strömung

Voices, Voices. Listen, my heart, as otherwise only
saints have listened: until the immense call
raised them off the ground; and they continued to kneel
and noticed nothing, these impossible creatures:
so completely they listened. Not that you could bear God's
voice, not by far. But hear that blowing,
its uninterrupted message forming from silence.
Now it roars toward you from those who died young.
Wherever you entered, in churches in Rome or Naples,
didn't their fate quietly speak to you?
Or an inscription solemnly commission itself to you,
as, not long ago, in that tablet in Santa Maria Formosa?
What do they ask of me? that I quietly remove the impression
of injustice, which at times impedes
a little their spirits' pure movement.

It's strange, of course, no longer to inhabit the earth,
no longer to practice barely learned customs,
not to give roses and other auspicious things
the meaning of a human future;
to be no longer what one was in infinitely
anxious hands, and even to put aside
one's own name like a broken toy.
Strange, to no longer keep wishing our wishes. Strange,
to see elements, once related, flutter
loosely in space. And being dead is toilsome,
and full of the retrieving needed if little by little
we're to feel a bit of eternity.—Yes, but the living
are mistaken to draw these distinctions so strictly.
Angels (it's said) often don't know if it's the living
they move among or the dead. The eternal current

reißt durch beide Bereiche alle Alter
immer mit sich und übertönt sie in beiden.

Schließlich brauchen sie uns nicht mehr, die Früheentrückten,
man entwöhnt sich des Irdischen sanft, wie man den Brüsten
milde der Mutter entwächst. Aber wir, die so große
Geheimnisse brauchen, denen aus Trauer so oft
seliger Fortschritt entspringt—: *könnten* wir sein ohne sie?
Ist die Sage umsonst, daß einst in der Klage um Linos
wagende erste Musik dürre Erstarrung durchdrang;
daß erst im erschrockenen Raum, dem ein beinah göttlicher
    Jüngling
plötzlich für immer enttrat, das Leere in jene
Schwingung geriet, die uns jetzt hinreißt und tröstet und hilft.

hurtles young and old down with it through both realms
forever, drowning out their voices in both.

In the end they no longer need us, these early whisked away;
gradually they disaccustom themselves to earth, as a child
gently grows away from the mother's breasts. But we, who
depend on such deep mysteries, whose blissful progress often
springs from sorrow—: *could* we exist without them?
Is the legend to no purpose that, long ago, in the mourning
    for Linos,
a daring first music broke through the benumbed
    desolation;
and in the terrified space that an almost godlike youth
suddenly quit forever, the void first resonated
with the vibration that now enraptures, consoles, and helps us.

DIE ZWEITE ELEGIE

Jeder Engel ist schrecklich. Und dennoch, weh mir,
ansing ich euch, fast tödliche Vögel der Seele,
wissend um euch. Wohin sind die Tage Tobiae,
da der Strahlendsten einer stand an der einfachen Haustür,
zur Reise ein wenig verkleidet und schon nicht mehr furchtbar;
(Jüngling dem Jüngling, wie er neugierig hinaussah).
Träte der Erzengel jetzt, der gefährliche, hinter den Sternen
eines Schrittes nur nieder und herwärts: hochauf-
schlagend erschlüg uns das eigene Herz. Wer seid ihr?

Frühe Geglückte, ihr Verwöhnten der Schöpfung,
Höhenzüge, morgenrötliche Grate
aller Erschaffung,—Pollen der blühenden Gottheit,
Gelenke des Lichtes, Gänge, Treppen, Throne,
Räume aus Wesen, Schilde aus Wonne, Tumulte
stürmisch entzückten Gefühls und plötzlich, einzeln,
Spiegel: die die entströmte eigene Schönheit
wiederschöpfen zurück in das eigene Antlitz.

Denn wir, wo wir fühlen, verflüchtigen; ach wir
atmen uns aus und dahin; von Holzglut zu Holzglut
geben wir schwächern Geruch. Da sagt uns wohl einer:
ja, du gehst mir ins Blut, dieses Zimmer, der Frühling
füllt sich mit dir . . . Was hilfts, er kann uns nicht halten,
wir schwinden in ihm und um ihn. Und jene, die schön sind,
o wer hält sie zurück? Unaufhörlich steht Anschein
auf in ihrem Gesicht und geht fort. Wie Tau von dem
　　Frühgras
hebt sich das Unsre von uns, wie die Hitze von einem
heißen Gericht. O Lächeln, wohin? O Aufschaun:

THE SECOND ELEGY

Every angel is terrifying. And yet, alas,
I sing to you, almost deadly birds of the soul,
even knowing about you. Where are the days of Tobias,
when a most-luminous one stood at a simple door,
partly disguised for the journey, no longer fearsome;
(how curiously he peered out, one youth at another).
But today if the archangel, the dangerous one, took even
one step down toward us from behind the stars: our own
high-beating heart would beat us to death. Who are you?

Early successes, pampered ones of creation,
lofty features, dawn-reddened ridges
of all createdness,—pollen of the blossoming godhead,
articulators of light, halls, staircases, thrones,
spaces of essence, shields of ecstasy, tumultuous
stormily-rapturous emotion, and suddenly, taken singly,
mirrors: scooping their own outstreamed
beauty back into their faces again.

But we, when we feel, pass off in vapor: we
breathe ourselves out and beyond; from ember to ember
we yield a weaker scent. Someone might say to us:
"Yes, you're in my blood, this room, the springtime
fills itself with you . . ." but it's no use, he can't hold us,
we disappear in and around him. And the beautiful,
could anyone hold them here? Semblance continually rises
into their faces and departs. Like dew from morning grass,
what is ours fumes away, like heat from a
warm dish. O smile, whereto? O upturned look:

neue, warme, entgehende Welle des Herzens——;
weh mir: wir *sinds* doch. Schmeckt denn der Weltraum,
in den wir uns lösen, nach uns? Fangen die Engel
wirklich nur Ihriges auf, ihnen Entströmtes,
oder ist manchmal, wie aus Versehen, ein wenig
unseres Wesens dabei? Sind wir in ihre
Züge soviel nur gemischt wie das Vage in die Gesichter
schwangerer Frauen? Sie merken es nicht in dem Wirbel
ihrer Rückkehr zu sich. (Wie sollten sie's merken.)

Liebende könnten, verstünden sie's, in der Nachtluft
wunderlich reden. Denn es scheint, daß uns alles
verheimlicht. Siehe, die Bäume *sind;* die Häuser,
die wir bewohnen, bestehn noch. Wir nur
ziehen allem vorbei wie ein luftiger Austausch.
Und alles ist einig, uns zu verschweigen, halb als
Schande vielleicht und halb als unsägliche Hoffnung.

Liebende, euch, ihr in einander Genügten,
frag ich nach uns. Ihr greift euch. Habt ihr Beweise?
Seht, mir geschiehts, daß meine Hände einander
inne werden oder daß mein gebrauchtes
Gesicht in ihnen sich schont. Das giebt mir ein wenig
Empfindung. Doch wer wagte darum schon zu *sein?*
Ihr aber, die ihr im Entzücken des anderen
zunehmt, bis er euch überwältigt
anfleht: nicht *mehr*——; die ihr unter den Händen
euch reichlicher werdet wie Traubenjahre;
die ihr manchmal vergeht, nur weil der andre
ganz überhand nimmt: euch frag ich nach uns. Ich weiß,

new, warm, escaping wave of the heart—;
alas, this is what we are. Does the space
we dissolve into taste of us? Do the angels take back
only what's theirs, what has streamed from them,
or do they catch, as if by accident, traces
of our being along with it? Are we mingled into their
features even so slightly as that vagueness in the faces
of pregnant women? They don't notice it, in the whirl
of their return to themselves. (How could they notice it?)

If lovers knew about this, how wondrously they could speak
in the night air. But it seems everything
keeps us in the dark. Look, the trees *are*; the houses
we live in still stand. We alone
go past them like an exchange of vapors.
And things conspire to tell us nothing, half
in shame, perhaps, half in unspoken hope.

Lovers, you who are sufficient each unto the other,
I ask you about us. You touch each other. But where's your proof?
Look, it sometimes happens that my hands become
aware of each other, or my worn
face takes comfort in them. That gives me a slight
sensation. But who would venture *existing*, just for that?
You, though, who increase in each other's
rapture, until the other, overwhelmed, begs
you: "No more"; you who under the other's hands
grow more abundant, like grapes in great years,
you, who all but faint away at times, only because the other
so fully prevails: You, I ask you about us. I know

ihr berührt euch so selig, weil die Liebkosung verhält,
weil die Stelle nicht schwindet, die ihr, Zärtliche,
zudeckt; weil ihr darunter das reine
Dauern verspürt. So versprecht ihr euch Ewigkeit fast
von der Umarmung. Und doch, wenn ihr der ersten
Blicke Schrecken besteht und die Sehnsucht am Fenster,
und den ersten gemeinsamen Gang, *ein* Mal durch den
        Garten:
Liebende, *seid* ihrs dann noch? Wenn ihr einer dem andern
euch an den Mund hebt und ansetzt—: Getränk an Getränk:
o wie entgeht dann der Trinkende seltsam der Handlung.

Erstaunte euch nicht auf attischen Stelen die Vorsicht
menschlicher Geste? war nicht Liebe und Abschied
so leicht auf die Schultern gelegt, als wär es aus anderm
Stoffe gemacht als bei uns? Gedenkt euch der Hände,
wie sie drucklos beruhen, obwohl in den Torsen die Kraft
        steht.
Diese Beherrschten wußten damit: so weit sind wirs,
dieses ist unser, uns *so* zu berühren; stärker
stemmen die Götter uns an. Doch dies ist Sache der Götter.

Fänden auch wir ein reines, verhaltenes, schmales
Menschliches, einen unseren Streifen Fruchtlands
zwischen Strom und Gestein. Denn das eigene Herz
        übersteigt uns
noch immer wie jene. Und wir können ihm nicht mehr
nachschaun in Bilder, die es besänftigen, noch in
göttliche Körper, in denen es größer sich mäßigt.

you touch so blissfully because, for you, the caress lasts,
because the place that you touch, tender ones, doesn't
disappear, because under your hands you feel pure
duration. So you promise each other eternity
almost, from your embrace. Once past the terror
of first glances, though, and the longing at the window
and the first walk, once, through the garden together:
lovers, are you still who you were? When you lift yourselves,
one to the other and touch lips—: drink upon drink:
oh, how strangely the drinker is missing from the act.

Weren't you amazed by the restraint in the human gestures
on Attic steles? weren't love and farewell
laid lightly on their shoulders, as if made of
other material than among us? Remember the hands,
how they rest without pressure, though there is power in the
    torsos.
These self-mastered ones knew: "We've come this far,
touching each other in this way, this is ours. The gods press
against us harder. But that is for the gods."

If only we could find a pure, reserved, narrow
bit of the human, our own strip of fertile land
between river and rock. For our heart still
overreaches us, just as theirs did them. And no longer
can we gaze back after it in images, which calm it, or
in godlike bodies where more grandly it tempers itself.

DIE DRITTE ELEGIE

Eines ist, die Geliebte zu singen. Ein anderes, wehe,
jenen verborgenen schuldigen Fluß-Gott des Bluts.
Den sie von weitem erkennt, ihren Jüngling, was weiß er
selbst von dem Herren der Lust, der aus dem Einsamen oft,
ehe das Mädchen noch linderte, oft auch als wäre sie nicht,
ach, von welchem Unkenntlichen triefend, das Gotthaupt
aufhob, aufrufend die Nacht zu unendlichem Aufruhr.
O des Blutes Neptun, o sein furchtbarer Dreizack.
O der dunkele Wind seiner Brust aus gewundener Muschel.
Horch, wie die Nacht sich muldet und höhlt. Ihr Sterne,
stammt nicht von euch des Liebenden Lust zu dem Antlitz
seiner Geliebten? Hat er die innige Einsicht
in ihr reines Gesicht nicht aus dem reinen Gestirn?

Du nicht hast ihm, wehe, nicht seine Mutter
hat ihm die Bogen der Braun so zur Erwartung gespannt.
Nicht an dir, ihn fühlendes Mädchen, an dir nicht
bog seine Lippe sich zum fruchtbarern Ausdruck.
Meinst du wirklich, ihn hätte dein leichter Auftritt
also erschüttert, du, die wandelt wie Frühwind?
Zwar du erschrakst ihm das Herz; doch ältere Schrecken
stürzten in ihn bei dem berührenden Anstoß.
Ruf ihn . . . du rufst ihn nicht ganz aus dunkelem Umgang.
Freilich, er *will*, er entspringt; erleichtert gewöhnt er
sich in dein heimliches Herz und nimmt und beginnt sich.
Aber begann er sich je?
Mutter, *du* machtest ihn klein, du warst, die ihn anfing;

THE THIRD ELEGY

It's one thing to sing the beloved. Another, beware,
that hidden guilty river god of the blood.
He, whom she can recognize from afar, her youthful lover,
    what does he
know of the lord of pleasures, who often, out of this lonely one,
before the girl could ease him, and often as if she didn't exist,
oh, dripping with what unrecognizable stuff, lifted
the god-head, rousing the night to infinite uproar.
O Neptune of the blood, O his terrible trident.
O dark wind in his breast out of the whorled conch.
Listen how the night troughs and hollows itself. You stars,
wasn't the lover's delight in his beloved's face
inspired by you; his intimate insight into
her pure countenance, by the pure constellations?

It wasn't you, alas, nor was it his mother,
who spanned his eyebrows into such expectancy.
Nor was it on you, girl holding him, not on your
mouth, that his lips curved into their fruitful fullness.
Do you really imagine your light entrance
could have convulsed him so, you who move like a dawn breeze?
Yes, you shocked his heart; but older terrors
swarmed into him at the slight push of your touch.
Call him . . . but you can't, not all the way back from those
    dark consorts.
Of course he wants to, he escapes; he settles, relieved,
in your intimate heart, and takes and begins himself over.
But did he begin himself, ever?
Mother, *you* made him small, it was you who began him;

dir war er neu, du beugtest über die neuen
Augen die freundliche Welt und wehrtest der fremden.
Wo, ach, hin sind die Jahre, da du ihm einfach
mit der schlanken Gestalt wallendes Chaos vertratst?
Vieles verbargst du ihm so; das nächtlich-verdächtige Zimmer
machtest du harmlos, aus deinem Herzen voll Zuflucht
mischtest du menschlichern Raum seinem Nacht-Raum hinzu.
Nicht in die Finsternis, nein, in dein näheres Dasein
hast du das Nachtlicht gestellt, und es schien wie aus
    Freundschaft.
Nirgends ein Knistern, das du nicht lächelnd erklärtest,
so als wüßtest du längst, *wann* sich die Diele benimmt . . .
Und er horchte und linderte sich. So vieles vermochte
zärtlich dein Aufstehn; hinter den Schrank trat
hoch im Mantel sein Schicksal, und in die Falten des Vorhangs
paßte, die leicht sich verschob, seine unruhige Zukunft.

Und er selbst, wie er lag, der Erleichterte, unter
schläfernden Lidern deiner leichten Gestaltung
Süße lösend in den gekosteten Vorschlaf—:
schien ein Gehüteter . . . Aber *innen*: wer wehrte,
hinderte innen in ihm die Fluten der Herkunft?
Ach, da *war* keine Vorsicht im Schlafenden; schlafend,
aber träumend, aber in Fiebern: wie er sich ein-ließ.
Er, der Neue, Scheuende, wie er verstrickt war,
mit des innern Geschehns weiterschlagenden Ranken
schon zu Mustern verschlungen, zu würgendem Wachstum,
    zu tierhaft

he was new to you, you bent over his new
eyes the friendly world, and shut out the hostile.
Oh, where are the years when you interposed
your slender figure between him and the seething chaos?
How much you hid from him: the room, nightly suspect,
you made harmless, out of your heart's refuge
you mingled a more human space into the space of his night.
Not in the dark, but in your nearer presence,
you placed the night lamp, gleaming as in friendship.
Nowhere a creak that you couldn't explain, with a smile,
as if you'd long known just when each floorboard would
        act up . . .
And he listened and was soothed. So much it availed,
your coming to him at night; his destiny, tall in its cloak,
        stepped back
behind the cupboard, and his unquiet future, easily shifting,
fitted itself into the folds of the curtain.

And he himself, lying there, relieved, under
eyelids you had so easily made heavy, infusing
your sweetness into the delicious beginnings of sleep—:
seemed protected . . . But within: who could fend off,
who could divert within him the deluge of origin?
Ah, there *was* no caution in this sleeper; sleeping
but dreaming, but feverish; how he let himself in for it.
So new and shy, how he grew entangled
in the spreading tendrils of these inner events,
that soon twined into patterns, choking growths, stalking

jagenden Formen. Wie er sich hingab—. Liebte.
Liebte sein Inneres, seines Inneren Wildnis,
diesen Urwald in ihm, auf dessen stummem Gestürztsein
lichtgrün sein Herz stand. Liebte. Verließ es, ging die
eigenen Wurzeln hinaus in gewaltigen Ursprung,
wo seine kleine Geburt schon überlebt war. Liebend
stieg er hinab in das ältere Blut, in die Schluchten,
wo das Furchtbare lag, noch satt von den Vätern. Und jedes
Schreckliche kannte ihn, blinzelte, war wie verständigt.
Ja, das Entsetzliche lächelte . . . Selten
hast du so zärtlich gelächelt, Mutter. Wie sollte
er es nicht lieben, da es ihm lächelte. *Vor* dir
hat ers geliebt, denn, da du ihn trugst schon,
war es im Wasser gelöst, das den Keimenden leicht macht.

Siehe, wir lieben nicht, wie die Blumen, aus einem
einzigen Jahr; uns steigt, wo wir lieben,
unvordenklicher Saft in die Arme. O Mädchen,
dies: daß wir liebten *in* uns, nicht Eines, ein Künftiges, sondern
das zahllos Brauende; nicht ein einzelnes Kind,
sondern die Väter, die wie Trümmer Gebirgs
uns im Grunde beruhn; sondern das trockene Flußbett
einstiger Mütter—; sondern die ganze
lautlose Landschaft unter dem wolkigen oder
reinen Verhängnis—: *dies* kam dir, Mädchen, zuvor.

Und du selber, was weißt du—, du locktest
Vorzeit empor in dem Liebenden. Welche Gefühle
wühlten herauf aus entwandelten Wesen. Welche

predatory forms. How he gave himself up—. Loved.
Loved what was within, his inner wilderness,
the primeval forest in him, in whose mute downfall
his heart stood light green. Loved. Then left, passed through his
own roots back out again into mighty origin
where his small birth had already been outlived. Loving,
he descended into the elder blood, into ravines
where ogres still lay, gorged with the fathers. Where everything
terrible, recognizing him, winked knowingly.
Yes, and the ghastly smiled . . . Rarely
have you smiled as tenderly, Mother. How could
he help loving it, when it smiled at him. Before you,
he loved it, for even as you carried him it was already
dissolved in the waters bearing lightly the embryo.

See, we don't love like the flowers, all in a
single year; for us, when we love, immemorial
sap rises into our arms. O you girl,
this: that far back within us, we loved, not one thing, not a
    thing in the future, but
all the innumerable brewing; not a particular child,
but the fathers lying in our depths like rubble
of wrecked mountains; but also the dry riverbeds
of former mothers—; but also the entire
silent landscape under a clouded or
clear fate—: girl, all this came before you.

And you yourself, what do you know—, you who lured
primordial time up into your lover. What passions
burrowed up into him from long-gone beings. What

Frauen haßten dich da. Was für finstere Männer
regtest du auf im Geäder des Jünglings? Tote
Kinder wollten zu dir . . . O leise, leise,
tu ein liebes vor ihm, ein verläßliches Tagwerk,—führ ihn
nah an den Garten heran, gieb ihm der Nächte
Übergewicht . . . . . .

          Verhalt ihn . . . . . .

women hated you in him. What shadowy men
did you arouse in his young veins? Dead
children reached out to you . . . Oh softly, softly,
do something loving before him, some faithful daytime
    task,—lead him
up close to the garden, give him what outweighs the
    heaviness
of the nights . . . . . .
                Hold him here . . . . . .

DIE VIERTE ELEGIE

O Bäume Lebens, o wann winterlich?
Wir sind nicht einig. Sind nicht wie die Zug-
vögel verständigt. Überholt und spät,
so drängen wir uns plötzlich Winden auf
und fallen ein auf teilnahmslosen Teich.
Blühn und verdorrn ist uns zugleich bewußt.
Und irgendwo gehn Löwen noch und wissen,
solang sie herrlich sind, von keiner Ohnmacht.

Uns aber, wo wir Eines meinen, ganz,
ist schon des andern Aufwand fühlbar. Feindschaft
ist uns das Nächste. Treten Liebende
nicht immerfort an Ränder, eins im andern,
die sich versprachen Weite, Jagd und Heimat.
    Da wird für eines Augenblickes Zeichnung
ein Grund von Gegenteil bereitet, mühsam,
daß wir sie sähen; denn man ist sehr deutlich
mit uns. Wir kennen den Kontur
des Fühlens nicht: nur, was ihn formt von außen.
    Wer saß nicht bang vor seines Herzens Vorhang?
Der schlug sich auf: die Szenerie war Abschied.
Leicht zu verstehen. Der bekannte Garten,
und schwankte leise: dann erst kam der Tänzer.
Nicht *der*. Genug! Und wenn er auch so leicht tut,
er ist verkleidet und er wird ein Bürger
und geht durch seine Küche in die Wohnung.
    Ich will nicht diese halbgefüllten Masken,
lieber die Puppe. Die ist voll. Ich will
den Balg aushalten und den Draht und ihr

THE FOURTH ELEGY

O trees of life, when does your winter come?
We're not in accord. Not attuned, like
the migrating birds. Overtaken and late,
we abruptly crowd ourselves on a wind
and come down on some uncaring pond.
We're conscious of blossoming and withering both at
     once.
And somewhere lions rove, all unaware,
while still in their splendor, of any weakness.

But we, giving ourselves to one thing,
feel it's at the expense of another. Conflict
is our nature. Don't lovers step up to
boundary lines, each in the other, all the time,
they who promised each other wide open spaces, hunting,
     and a home.
   For a moment's sketch, a contrasting
ground is laboriously prepared, so that
we can see them: in this way things are made
clear to us. Of the contours of emotions
we know only what forms them from without.
     Who hasn't waited anxiously before the heart's curtain?
It went up: the stage-set was parting.
Easy to understand. The same old garden,
undulating slightly: and then came the dancer.
Not *him*! Enough! Lightly as he leaps,
he's in disguise, and soon reverts to
a common citizen who enters his place through the kitchen.
   I don't want these half-filled masks;
give me the puppet. It's full. Gladly will I put up with
the sewing-bag body, the wires, and that face

Gesicht aus Aussehn. Hier. Ich bin davor.
Wenn auch die Lampen ausgehn, wenn mir auch
gesagt wird: Nichts mehr—, wenn auch von der Bühne
das Leere herkommt mit dem grauen Luftzug,
wenn auch von meinen stillen Vorfahrn keiner
mehr mit mir dasitzt, keine Frau, sogar
der Knabe nicht mehr mit dem braunen Schielaug:
Ich bleibe dennoch. Es giebt immer Zuschaun.

Hab ich nicht recht? Du, der um mich so bitter
das Leben schmeckte, meines kostend, Vater,
den ersten trüben Aufguß meines Müssens,
da ich heranwuchs, immer wieder kostend
und, mit dem Nachgeschmack so fremder Zukunft
beschäftigt, prüftest mein beschlagnes Aufschaun,—
der du, mein Vater, seit du tot bist, oft
in meiner Hoffnung, innen in mir, Angst hast,
und Gleichmut, wie ihn Tote haben, Reiche
von Gleichmut, aufgiebst für mein bißchen Schicksal,
hab ich nicht recht? Und ihr, hab ich nicht recht,
die ihr mich liebtet für den kleinen Anfang
Liebe zu euch, von dem ich immer abkam,
weil mir der Raum in eurem Angesicht,
da ich ihn liebte, überging in Weltraum,
in dem ihr nicht mehr wart . . . . : wenn mir zumut ist,
zu warten vor der Puppenbühne, nein,
so völlig hinzuschaun, daß, um mein Schauen
am Ende aufzuwiegen, dort als Spieler
ein Engel hinmuß, der die Bälge hochreißt.
Engel und Puppe: dann ist endlich Schauspiel.
Dann kommt zusammen, was wir immerfort
entzwein, indem wir da sind. Dann entsteht
aus unsern Jahreszeiten erst der Umkreis

made of mere show. Here. I'm before it.
Even if they put out the lights, even if they
tell me: "That's it," even if the emptiness gusts
toward me from the stage on a gray draft,
even if not one of my quiet ancestors,
no woman, not even the boy with the
paralyzed brown eye, will sit with me:
I'll stay anyway. There's always spectating.

Am I wrong? You to whom life tasted
so bitter once you'd tasted mine, Father,
those first turbid infusions in me of the imperative,
you who, as I grew older, kept on tasting,
and, concerned by the aftertaste of so strange a future,
studied my clouded upward gaze,—
you, my father, who often, within me, in my hope,
fear for me, now that you're dead,
and trade some of your serenity, such as the dead have,
all those kingdoms of serenity, for my bit of destiny,
have I got it right? And you, am I not right,
all you who loved me for my first beginning
of love for you, love from which I always retreated,
because the space within your faces changed,
when I loved it, into an infinite space,
where you no longer were. . . . : when the mood takes me,
to wait before the puppet stage, or rather, watch it
so perfectly that finally, to offset
my stare, an angel appears, as puppeteer,
and jerks the stuffed pelts into action.
Angel and puppet: at last we have a spectacle.
Then come together what we constantly separate
simply by existing. And only then

des ganzen Wandelns. Über uns hinüber
spielt dann der Engel. Sieh, die Sterbenden,
sollten sie nicht vermuten, wie voll Vorwand
das alles ist, was wir hier leisten. Alles
ist nicht es selbst. O Stunden in der Kindheit,
da hinter den Figuren mehr als nur
Vergangnes war und vor uns nicht die Zukunft.
Wir wuchsen freilich und wir drängten manchmal,
bald groß zu werden, denen halb zulieb,
die andres nicht mehr hatten, als das Großsein.
Und waren doch, in unserem Alleingehn,
mit Dauerndem vergnügt und standen da
im Zwischenraume zwischen Welt und Spielzeug,
an einer Stelle, die seit Anbeginn
gegründet war für einen reinen Vorgang.

Wer zeigt ein Kind, so wie es steht? Wer stellt
es ins Gestirn und giebt das Maß des Abstands
ihm in die Hand? Wer macht den Kindertod
aus grauem Brot, das hart wird,—oder läßt
ihn drin im runden Mund, so wie den Gröps
von einem schönen Apfel? . . . . . . Mörder sind
leicht einzusehen. Aber dies: den Tod,
den ganzen Tod, noch *vor* dem Leben so
sanft zu enthalten und nicht bös zu sein,
ist unbeschreiblich.

can we see, in our seasons, the full cycle
of all changes. Then the angel
will play, above and beyond us. Shouldn't at least
the dying have guessed how much pretense
goes into all we accomplish here. Nothing
is itself. O hours of childhood,
when behind each of those figures lay
more than the past, and before us, not the future.
We were growing up, of course, impatient at times
to grow up more quickly, half to oblige those
who had nothing to show for having grown up.
And yet, when left on our own, what we liked
was what did not change, and there we stood
in the space between world and toy,
a place that had from the beginning
been consecrated for a pure event.

Who shows a child as he really is? Who places
him among the stars and puts the measuring stick of separation
into his hands? Who makes the child's death
out of gray bread, which hardens,—or leaves
it inside the rounded mouth like the core
of a beautiful apple? . . . . . . Murderers are
easy to understand. But this, though: death,
all of death, even before life has begun,
to hold it all so gently and without rancor,
this is beyond description.

DIE FÜNFTE ELEGIE

Wer aber *sind* sie, sag mir, die Fahrenden, diese ein wenig
Flüchtigern noch als wir selbst, die dringend von früh an
wringt ein *wem*, *wem* zu Liebe
niemals zufriedener Wille? Sondern er wringt sie,
biegt sie, schlingt sie und schwingt sie,
wirft sie und fängt sie zurück; wie aus geölter,
glatterer Luft kommen sie nieder
auf dem verzehrten, von ihrem ewigen
Aufsprung dünneren Teppich, diesem verlorenen
Teppich im Weltall.
Aufgelegt wie ein Pflaster, als hätte der Vorstadt-
Himmel der Erde dort wehe getan.

                             Und kaum dort,
aufrecht, da und gezeigt: des Dastehns
großer Anfangsbuchstab . . . , schon auch, die stärksten
Männer, rollt sie wieder, zum Scherz, der immer
kommende Griff, wie August der Starke bei Tisch
einen zinnenen Teller.

Ach und um diese
Mitte, die Rose des Zuschauns:
blüht und entblättert. Um diesen
Stampfer, den Stempel, den von dem eignen
blühenden Staub getroffnen, zur Scheinfrucht
wieder der Unlust befruchteten, ihrer
niemals bewußten,—glänzend mit dünnster
Oberfläche leicht scheinlächelnden Unlust.

THE FIFTH ELEGY

But who are they, tell me, these itinerants, more
fugitive even than we ourselves, urgently twisted from
an early age, why, for whose sake?
by a never-content will. And still it wrings them,
bends them, slings them and swings them,
flings them and catches them; as if dropping through oiled,
more slippery air they come down
on the bitten carpet frazzled thin from
the endless hard leap-offs, this carpet
wandering in infinite space.
Laid down here like a bandage, as if the sky
of the city outskirts just here had injured the earth.
                                    And scarcely in place,
upright, on display: the capitalized first
letter of *Dastehn* . . . , and already the grip
returns, rolling them up yet again, for fun, these strongest
of men, like Augustus the Strong at table
crushing a pewter plate.

Ah, and around this
center, the rose of onlooking:
blossoms and sheds. Around this
pestle, the pistil, pollinated by its own
blossom's dust to form
the next specious fruit of unpleasure,
alert to nothing—its thin skin
gleaming with listless false smiles.

Dastehn: "Standing there." The tumblers in Picasso's painting "La
Famille des Saltimbanques," which this elegy is partly based upon,
are arranged in such a way as to form the letter "D."

Da: der welke, faltige Stemmer,
der alte, der nur noch trommelt,
eingegangen in seiner gewaltigen Haut, als hätte sie früher
zwei Männer enthalten, und einer
läge nun schon auf dem Kirchhof, und er überlebte den andern,
taub und manchmal ein wenig
wirr, in der verwitweten Haut.

Aber der junge, der Mann, als wär er der Sohn eines Nackens
und einer Nonne: prall und strammig erfüllt
mit Muskeln und Einfalt.

Oh ihr,
die ein Leid, das noch klein war,
einst als Spielzeug bekam, in einer seiner
langen Genesungen . . . .

Du, der mit dem Aufschlag,
wie nur Früchte ihn kennen, unreif,
täglich hundertmal abfällt vom Baum der gemeinsam
erbauten Bewegung (der, rascher als Wasser, in wenig
Minuten Lenz, Sommer und Herbst hat)—
abfällt und anprallt ans Grab:
manchmal, in halber Pause, will dir ein liebes
Antlitz entstehn hinüber zu deiner selten
zärtlichen Mutter; doch an deinen Körper verliert sich,
der es flächig verbraucht, das schüchtern
kaum versuchte Gesicht . . . Und wieder
klatscht der Mann in die Hand zu dem Ansprung, und eh dir
jemals ein Schmerz deutlicher wird in der Nähe des immer
trabenden Herzens, kommt das Brennen der Fußsohln
ihm, seinem Ursprung, zuvor mit ein paar dir

Here: the wilted, wrinkled strong man,
the old one, who only drums now,
shrunken in his huge hide, which looks to have
once contained two men—and one
lay already in the graveyard, and this one had outlived him,
deaf, and sometimes
a bit confused in his widowed skin.

But that young man, like the son of a neck
and a nun: firm and robustly packed
with muscles and innocence.

Oh you,
once given as a plaything to a Sorrow
that was still small, in one of its
prolonged convalescences. . . .

And you, who fall with the thud
only unripe fruit know,
a hundred times daily, out of a tree of mutually
built-up motion (which, swifter than a waterfall,
speeds through spring, summer, and fall)—
fall, and knock against the grave:
at times, in almost a pause, a loving look
wants to rise in you, over and across to your seldom
tender mother; but this shy, scarcely attempted
mien loses itself to your body,
which uses it up on itself . . . And again
the man claps his hands for the jump-off, and just
before you register the pain near your steadily
pounding heart, the smarting footsoles
intervene, back where they started, and chase a few

rasch in die Augen gejagten leiblichen Tränen.
Und dennoch, blindlings,
das Lächeln . . . . .

Engel! o nimms, pflücks, das kleinblütige Heilkraut.
Schaff eine Vase, verwahrs! Stells unter jene, uns *noch* nicht
offenen Freuden; in lieblicher Urne
rühms mit blumiger schwungiger Aufschrift:
>*Subrisio Saltat.*<.

Du dann, Liebliche,
du, von den reizendsten Freuden
stumm Übersprungne. Vielleicht sind
deine Fransen glücklich für dich—,
oder über den jungen
prallen Brüsten die grüne metallene Seide
fühlt sich unendlich verwöhnt und entbehrt nichts.
Du,
immerfort anders auf alle des Gleichgewichts schwankende
Waagen
hingelegte Marktfrucht des Gleichmuts,
öffentlich unter den Schultern.

Wo, o *wo* ist der Ort—ich trag ihn im Herzen—,
wo sie noch lange nicht *konnten*, noch von einander
abfieln, wie sich bespringende, nicht recht
paarige Tiere;—
wo die Gewichte noch schwer sind;
wo noch von ihren vergeblich
wirbelnden Stäben die Teller
torkeln. . . . .

bodily tears into your eyes.
And yet, blindly,
the smile. . . . .

Angel! Oh, take it, pluck it, this small-flowered healing herb.
Fashion a vase, put it in. Shelve it among joys not yet
revealed to us; and across this shapely urn
praise it with a flowery, flowing inscription:

Subrisio Saltat.

And now you, lovely one,
leapt over without a word by the
sweetest of joys. Perhaps
at least your fringes are happy—,
or the metallic green silk
drawn over your firm youthful breasts
feels utterly indulged and in need of nothing.
You,
marketable fruit of equipoise, always positioned in new ways
on the swaying scale pans of equilibrium,
there, just below the shoulders, for public viewing.

Where, oh where is the place—I carry it in my heart—,
where for a long time they *couldn't*,
and fell away from each other, like animals mounting not quite
suitable mates:—
where the weights are still heavy;
where from the vainly twirling staves
the plates still go reeling
away. . . . .

Subrisio Saltat: *Subrisio Saltatorum* (the smiling of the tumblers, the
artistes), abbreviated, as on the label of an apothecary's jar.

Und plötzlich in diesem mühsamen Nirgends, plötzlich
die unsägliche Stelle, wo sich das reine Zuwenig
unbegreiflich verwandelt—, umspringt
in jenes leere Zuviel.
Wo die vielstellige Rechnung
zahlenlos aufgeht.

Plätze, o Platz in Paris, unendlicher Schauplatz,
wo die Modistin, *Madame Lamort,*
die ruhlosen Wege der Erde, endlose Bänder,
schlingt und windet und neue aus ihnen
Schleifen erfindet, Rüschen, Blumen, Kokarden, künstliche
     Früchte—, alle
unwahr gefärbt,—für die billigen
Winterhüte des Schicksals.
. . . .

Engel!: Es wäre ein Platz, den wir nicht wissen, und dorten,
auf unsäglichem Teppich, zeigten die Liebenden, die's hier
bis zum Können nie bringen, ihre kühnen
hohen Figuren des Herzschwungs,
ihre Türme aus Lust, ihre
längst, wo Boden nie war, nur an einander
lehnenden Leitern, bebend,—und *könntens,*
vor den Zuschauern rings, unzähligen lautlosen Toten:
     Würfen die dann ihre letzten, immer ersparten,
immer verborgenen, die wir nicht kennen, ewig
gültigen Münzen des Glücks vor das endlich
wahrhaft lächelnde Paar auf gestilltem
Teppich?

And suddenly, in this effortful nowhere, suddenly
the inexpressible spot where the pure too-little
mysteriously transforms—, flips round
into the empty too-much.
And the whole many-digited calculation
comes out to zero.

Squares, O square in Paris, never-ending scene,
in which the modiste Madame Lamort
loops and twists the restless paths of earth,
endless ribbons, inventing new bows,
frills, flowers, cockades, artificial fruits—, all
dyed all wrong,—for the cheap
winter hats of fate.
. . . .

Angel!: If there were a place we know nothing of, and there,
on some ineffable carpet, beloveds who never
accomplished it here could show at last their
heart-swings' bold high-flying figures,
their towers of rapture, their ladders
leaning a long time only on each other
on ground that never existed—and, trembling, *could do it*,
before spectators crowded round, the innumerable
     speechless dead:
   Would these then toss down their last, forever saved up,
ever hidden away, unknown to us, eternally
valid coins of happiness, before the finally
truly smiling pair on the quietened
carpet?

DIE SECHSTE ELEGIE

Feigenbaum, seit wie lange schon ists mir bedeutend,
wie du die Blüte beinah ganz überschlägst
und hinein in die zeitig entschlossene Frucht,
ungerühmt, drängst dein reines Geheimnis.
Wie der Fontäne Rohr treibt dein gebognes Gezweig
abwärts den Saft und hinan: und er springt aus dem Schlaf,
fast nicht erwachend, ins Glück seiner süßesten Leistung.
Sieh: wie der Gott in den Schwan.

      . . . . . . Wir aber verweilen,
ach, uns rühmt es zu blühn, und ins verspätete Innre
unserer endlichen Frucht gehn wir verraten hinein.
Wenigen steigt so stark der Andrang des Handelns,
daß sie schon anstehn und glühn in der Fülle des Herzens,
wenn die Verführung zum Blühn wie gelinderte Nachtluft
ihnen die Jugend des Munds, ihnen die Lider berührt:
Helden vielleicht und den frühe Hinüberbestimmten,
denen der gärtnernde Tod anders die Adern verbiegt.
Diese stürzen dahin: dem eigenen Lächeln
sind sie voran, wie das Rossegespann in den milden
muldigen Bildern von Karnak dem siegenden König.

Wunderlich nah ist der Held doch den jugendlich Toten.
    Dauern
ficht ihn nicht an. Sein Aufgang ist Dasein; beständig
nimmt er sich fort und tritt ins veränderte Sternbild
seiner steten Gefahr. Dort fänden ihn wenige. Aber,
das uns finster verschweigt, das plötzlich begeisterte Schicksal
singt ihn hinein in den Sturm seiner aufrauschenden Welt.
Hör ich doch keinen wie *ihn*. Auf einmal durchgeht mich
mit der strömenden Luft sein verdunkelter Ton.

THE SIXTH ELEGY

Fig tree, for how long have I found meaning
in the way you almost skip the flowering
and thrust your pure mystery,
unsung, into the early set fruit.
Like the fountain's pipe, your dipping boughs
drive the sap down and then up: and it leaps
from sleep, into the bliss of its sweetest achievement.
See: like the god into the swan.

                                        . . . . . . But *we* hang back,
ah, we revel in the flowering, and enter the belated inner
space of our ultimate fruit already betrayed.
In just a few, the urge to act rises so powerfully
they are already waiting, aglow in their hearts' fullness,
when the temptation to blossom, like softened night air,
touches the youth of their mouths and their eyelids:
heroes perhaps, and those chosen to go over early,
whose veins gardening death has twisted differently.
These charge forward: ahead of
their own smiles, as the team of horses in the
low-relief carvings of Karnak precedes the victorious king.

How oddly akin is the hero to the early dead. Duration
doesn't interest him. For him, only ascent matters; steadfastly
he drives on and enters the altered constellation
of his constant danger. There few would find him. But
fate, which grimly shuts us in silence, suddenly inspired
sings him into the storm of his uproaring world.
I hear nobody like *him*. Suddenly his low tone
blows through me, borne on the streaming air.

Dann, wie verbärg ich mich gern vor der Sehnsucht: O wär ich,
wär ich ein Knabe und dürft es noch werden und säße
in die künftigen Arme gestützt und läse von Simson,
wie seine Mutter erst nichts und dann alles gebar.

War er nicht Held schon in dir, o Mutter, begann nicht
dort schon, in dir, seine herrische Auswahl?
Tausende brauten im Schoß und wollten *er* sein,
aber sieh: er ergriff und ließ aus—, wählte und konnte.
Und wenn er Säulen zerstieß, so wars, da er ausbrach
aus der Welt deines Leibs in die engere Welt, wo er weiter
wählte und konnte. O Mütter der Helden, o Ursprung
reißender Ströme! Ihr Schluchten, in die sich
hoch von dem Herzrand, klagend,
schon die Mädchen gestürzt, künftig die Opfer dem Sohn.

Denn hinstürmte der Held durch Aufenthalte der Liebe,
jeder hob ihn hinaus, jeder ihn meinende Herzschlag,
abgewendet schon, stand er am Ende der Lächeln,
    —anders.

Then how I'd like to hide from that yearning: "Oh, were I,
were I a boy again, still eligible to be one of them, leaning
on still childish arms, reading about Sampson,
how his mother bore first nothing and then all."

Wasn't he already a hero, inside you, Mother, hadn't his
imperious choosing already begun, inside you?
Thousands brewed in the womb wanting to be *him*,
but look: he picked up and discarded—, chose and prevailed.
And when he shattered the pillars, that was his breaking out
from the world of your body, into the narrower world, where
again he chose and prevailed. O mothers of heroes, O sources
of torrential rivers. Gorges into which, high from the
rim of the heart, young girls, lamenting,
threw themselves, sacrifices in advance to the son.

For when the hero stormed on through the bowers of love,
each heartbeat meant for him lifted him past itself;
already turned away, he stood at the end of the smiles,
        —different.

DIE SIEBENTE ELEGIE

Werbung nicht mehr, nicht Werbung, entwachsene Stimme,
sei deines Schreies Natur; zwar schrieest du rein wie der
    Vogel,
wenn ihn die Jahreszeit aufhebt, die steigende, beinah
    vergessend,
daß er ein kümmerndes Tier und nicht nur ein einzelnes
    Herz sei,
das sie ins Heitere wirft, in die innigen Himmel. Wie er, so
würbest du wohl, nicht minder—, daß, noch unsichtbar,
dich die Freundin erführ, die stille, in der eine Antwort
langsam erwacht und über dem Hören sich anwärmt,—
deinem erkühnten Gefühl die erglühte Gefühlin.

O und der Frühling begriffe—, da ist keine Stelle,
die nicht trüge den Ton der Verkündigung. Erst jenen kleinen
fragenden Auflaut, den, mit steigernder Stille,
weithin umschweigt ein reiner bejahender Tag.
Dann die Stufen hinan, Ruf-Stufen hinan, zum geträumten
Tempel der Zukunft—; dann den Triller, Fontäne,
die zu dem drängenden Strahl schon das Fallen zuvornimmt
im versprechlichen Spiel . . . . Und vor sich, den Sommer.

Nicht nur die Morgen alle des Sommers—, nicht nur
wie sie sich wandeln in Tag und strahlen vor Anfang.
Nicht nur die Tage, die zart sind um Blumen, und oben,
um die gestalteten Bäume, stark und gewaltig.
Nicht nur die Andacht dieser entfalteten Kräfte,
nicht nur die Wege, nicht nur die Wiesen im Abend,
nicht nur, nach spätem Gewitter, das atmende Klarsein,
nicht nur der nahende Schlaf und ein Ahnen, abends . . .

THE SEVENTH ELEGY

Wooing no more, not wooing, outgrown voice,
be the character of your cry; though it were pure as a bird's,
when the season, rising, lifts him, almost forgetting
he's an actual worrying creature and not just a heart
being flung into the brightness, the innermost heavens. You too
would woo, no less than he—, so that your quiet sweetheart,
in whom a response slowly awakens, might come to know you,
still invisible, and be aroused by way of listening,—
passion-mate of your emboldening passion.

Oh, and springtime would know it—, there's nowhere
that wouldn't carry the sound of that annunciation. First those
small, querying up-notes that a pure affirming day
hushes all around, from afar, in mounting stillness.
Then up steps, up call-steps, to the dreamed-of
temple of the future—; and then the trill, fountain
whose urgent jet bursts up through its falling
in a contest of promises. . . . And soon to come, the summer.

Not only all the mornings of summer—, not only
how they open into day, radiant in their beginning.
Not only the days, so gentle around flowers, and above,
around the structured trees, so strong and forceful.
Not only the fervor of these unfolded powers,
not only the paths, not only the meadows at sunset,
not only, after a late thunderstorm, the breathing clarity,
not only, at evening, approaching sleep and a presentiment . . .

sondern die Nächte! Sondern die hohen, des Sommers,
Nächte, sondern die Sterne, die Sterne der Erde.
O einst tot sein und sie wissen unendlich,
alle die Sterne: denn wie, wie, wie sie vergessen!

Siehe, da rief ich die Liebende. Aber nicht *sie* nur
käme . . . Es kämen aus schwächlichen Gräbern
Mädchen und ständen . . . Denn, wie beschränk ich,
wie, den gerufenen Ruf? Die Versunkenen suchen
immer noch Erde.—Ihr Kinder, ein hiesig
einmal ergriffenes Ding gälte für viele.
Glaubt nicht, Schicksal sei mehr, als das Dichte der Kindheit;
wie überholtet ihr oft den Geliebten, atmend,
atmend nach seligem Lauf, auf nichts zu, ins Freie.

Hiersein ist herrlich. Ihr wußtet es, Mädchen, *ihr* auch,
die ihr scheinbar entbehrtet, versank—, ihr, in den ärgsten
Gassen der Städte, Schwärende, oder dem Abfall
Offene. Denn eine Stunde war jeder, vielleicht nicht
ganz eine Stunde, ein mit den Maßen der Zeit kaum
Meßliches zwischen zwei Weilen—, da sie ein Dasein
hatte. Alles. Die Adern voll Dasein.
Nur, wir vergessen so leicht, was der lachende Nachbar
uns nicht bestätigt oder beneidet. Sichtbar
wollen wirs heben, wo doch das sichtbarste Glück uns
erst zu erkennen sich giebt, wenn wir es innen verwandeln.

Nirgends, Geliebte, wird Welt sein, als innen. Unser
Leben geht hin mit Verwandlung. Und immer geringer
schwindet das Außen. Wo einmal ein dauerndes Haus war,
schlägt sich erdachtes Gebild vor, quer, zu Erdenklichem

but the nights! But the immense nights of
summer, but the stars, the stars of the earth.
Oh, one day to be dead and to know them infinitely,
all the stars: for how, how, how could we forget them!

There, I've called the beloved. But not she alone
would come . . . Also girls out of loosely covered graves
would come and stand here . . . For how could I ever limit
the call, once called? For everyone who's buried
still searches for earth.—You children, even just one
earthly thing if truly grasped would make up for so many.
Don't think fate is more than the impenetrability of
    childhood;
how often you ran out ahead of your young man, panting,
panting, from that blissful run toward nothing, into the open.

Being here is glorious. You knew it, you girls, even you
who seemed to go wanting, who sank—, you, into
the most squalid streets of the city, festering, open to
garbage. For each of you had her hour, perhaps not
even an hour, but some span all but unmeasurable
as we measure time, between two moments—, when you
existed. Everything. Veins full of existence.
But we forget so easily what our laughing neighbor
neither notices nor envies us. We would raise it up
and show it, even though the most visible happiness
reveals itself only when we've transformed it within.

Nowhere, Beloved, will there be world but within. Our
lives pass in transformation. Into less and less
the external dwindles. Where once an enduring house stood,
a contrived structure now proposes itself, at odds with things,

völlig gehörig, als ständ es noch ganz im Gehirne.
Weite Speicher der Kraft schafft sich der Zeitgeist, gestaltlos
wie der spannende Drang, den er aus allem gewinnt.
Tempel kennt er nicht mehr. Diese, des Herzens,
     Verschwendung
sparen wir heimlicher ein. Ja, wo noch eins übersteht,
ein einst gebetetes Ding, ein gedientes, geknietes—,
hält es sich, so wie es ist, schon ins Unsichtbare hin.
Viele gewahrens nicht mehr, doch ohne den Vorteil,
daß sie's nun *innerlich* baun, mit Pfeilern und Statuen, größer!

Jede dumpfe Umkehr der Welt hat solche Enterbte,
denen das Frühere nicht und noch nicht das Nächste gehört.
Denn auch das Nächste ist weit für die Menschen. *Uns* soll
dies nicht verwirren; es stärke in uns die Bewahrung
der noch erkannten Gestalt.—Dies *stand* einmal unter
     Menschen,
mitten im Schicksal stands, im vernichtenden, mitten
im Nichtwissen-Wohin stand es, wie seiend, und bog
Sterne zu sich aus gesicherten Himmeln. Engel,
dir noch zeig ich es, *da!* in deinem Anschaun
steh es gerettet zuletzt, nun endlich aufrecht.
Säulen, Pylone, der Sphinx, das strebende Stemmen,
grau aus vergehender Stadt oder aus fremder, des Doms.

War es nicht Wunder? O staune, Engel, denn *wir* sinds,
wir, o du Großer, erzähls, daß wir solches vermochten, mein
     Atem
reicht für die Rühmung nicht aus. So haben wir dennoch
nicht die Räume versäumt, diese gewährenden, diese

completely conceptual, as if it still stood in the brain.
Our age builds enormous reservoirs of power, formless
as the tensing stress it extracts from everything.
It doesn't know temples anymore. Such heart's squanderings
we hoard up more secretly. Yes, whenever one survives,
a thing once venerated, served, knelt before—,
it starts tilting, just as it is, into the unseen.
Many can perceive it no longer, but without the gain
of rebuilding it within, with columns and statues, greater.

Each blind lurch of the world leaves its disinherited,
to whom no longer the past and not yet the future belong.
For humans, even what is nearest is far. This ought not to
confuse us; but strengthen us in safeguarding
the still-recognizable forms.—*This* once stood among us,
in the middle of fate it stood, among the annihilated, in the
    middle
of Not-knowing-where-to-next, it stood as if it belonged
    here, and bent
the stars down toward it from the secured heavens. Angel,
I'll show it to *you*: there! in your seeing
it stands, finally rescued, finally upright.
Pillars, pylons, Sphinx, the cathedral's striving
thrust, gray, out of a vanishing or alien city.

Wasn't it all a miracle? O marvel, angel, for it is we,
we, O you great one, tell them that we were capable of this,
    my breath's
too small for the praising. And so, after all, we didn't
fail to make use of these bountiful spaces, these spaces

unseren Räume. (Was müssen sie fürchterlich groß sein,
da sie Jahrtausende nicht unseres Fühlns überfülln.)
Aber ein Turm war groß, nicht wahr? O Engel, er war es,—
groß, auch noch neben dir? Chartres war groß—, und Musik
reichte noch weiter hinan und überstieg uns. Doch selbst nur
eine Liebende—, oh, allein am nächtlichen Fenster. . . .
reichte sie dir nicht ans Knie—?

                                  Glaub *nicht*, daß ich werbe.
Engel, und würb ich dich auch! Du kommst nicht. Denn
   mein
Anruf ist immer voll Hinweg; wider so starke
Strömung kannst du nicht schreiten. Wie ein gestreckter
Arm ist mein Rufen. Und seine zum Greifen
oben offene Hand bleibt vor dir
offen, wie Abwehr und Warnung,
Unfaßlicher, weitauf.

of *ours*. (How terrifyingly vast they must be,
if thousands of years of our feeling haven't overfilled them.)
But a tower was tall—wasn't it? O angel, it was,—
tall, even next to you? Chartres was immense—, and music
rose higher still and soared beyond us. Yet even only
one solitary girl in love—, oh, at night by her window. . . .
didn't she come up to your knee—?

                                   Don't imagine I'm wooing.
Angel, and even if I were! You do not come. For my
call to you is always filled with "away"; against this powerful
current you cannot advance. Like an outstretched
arm is my call. And its lifted hand, opened
to grasp, remains open before you,
as if to fend off and warn,
ungraspable one, wide open.

DIE ACHTE ELEGIE

Mit allen Augen sieht die Kreatur
das Offene. Nur unsre Augen sind
wie umgekehrt und ganz um sie gestellt
als Fallen, rings um ihren freien Ausgang.
Was draußen *ist*, wir wissens aus des Tiers
Antlitz allein; denn schon das frühe Kind
wenden wir um und zwingens, daß es rückwärts
Gestaltung sehe, nicht das Offne, das
im Tiergesicht so tief ist. Frei von Tod.
Ihn sehen wir allein; das freie Tier
hat seinen Untergang stets hinter sich
und vor sich Gott, und wenn es geht, so gehts
in Ewigkeit, so wie die Brunnen gehen.

    Wir haben nie, nicht einen einzigen Tag,
den reinen Raum vor uns, in den die Blumen
unendlich aufgehn. Immer ist es Welt
und niemals Nirgends ohne Nicht: das Reine,
Unüberwachte, das man atmet und
unendlich *weiß* und nicht begehrt. Als Kind
verliert sich eins im Stilln an dies und wird
gerüttelt. Oder jener stirbt und ists.
Denn nah am Tod sieht man den Tod nicht mehr
und starrt *hinaus*, vielleicht mit großem Tierblick.
Liebende, wäre nicht der andre, der
die Sicht verstellt, sind nah daran und staunen . . .
Wie aus Versehn ist ihnen aufgetan
hinter dem andern . . . Aber über ihn
kommt keiner fort, und wieder wird ihm Welt.
Der Schöpfung immer zugewendet, sehn

THE EIGHTH ELEGY

With all its eyes the creature
sees the open. Our eyes alone are
as if turned back, and placed all around,
like traps, encircling its free escape.
What *is* outside we know only
from the animal's face; and we even
twist the young child around and force it to look
at created things, not at the open
deep in the creature's face. Free from death.
But death we alone can see: the free animal
always has its demise behind it
and God before, and when it walks it walks
into eternity, like the flowing of a spring.
    We never, not for a single day, have
before us the pure space into which flowers
endlessly open. Always it is world,
and never nowhere without the no: that pure,
unsurveilled element one breathes and
infinitely knows, without desiring. As a child,
one may lose oneself to it in silence, and be
shaken back. Or die and *be* it.
For close to death, we stop seeing death,
and stare beyond, perhaps with the vast gaze of animals.
Lovers, if the other were not there,
obstructing the view, come near to it and marvel . . .
As if by oversight it opens up to each
behind the other . . . But neither can
get past, and once again it is world.
Always turned toward the created, we see

wir nur auf ihr die Spiegelung des Frein,
von uns verdunkelt. Oder daß ein Tier,
ein stummes, aufschaut, ruhig durch uns durch.
Dieses heißt Schicksal: gegenüber sein
und nichts als das und immer gegenüber.

Wäre Bewußtheit unsrer Art in dem
sicheren Tier, das uns entgegenzieht
in anderer Richtung—, riß es uns herum
mit seinem Wandel. Doch sein Sein ist ihm
unendlich, ungefaßt und ohne Blick
auf seinen Zustand, rein, so wie sein Ausblick.
Und wo wir Zukunft sehn, dort sieht es Alles
und sich in Allem und geheilt für immer.

Und doch ist in dem wachsam warmen Tier
Gewicht und Sorge einer großen Schwermut.
Denn ihm auch haftet immer an, was uns
oft überwältigt,—die Erinnerung,
als sei schon einmal das, wonach man drängt,
näher gewesen, treuer und sein Anschluß
unendlich zärtlich. Hier ist alles Abstand,
und dort wars Atem. Nach der ersten Heimat
ist ihm die zweite zwitterig und windig.
    O Seligkeit der *kleinen* Kreatur,
die immer *bleibt* im Schoße, der sie austrug;
o Glück der Mücke, die noch *innen* hüpft,
selbst wenn sie Hochzeit hat: denn Schoß ist Alles.
Und sieh die halbe Sicherheit des Vogels,
der beinah beides weiß aus seinem Ursprung,
als wär er eine Seele der Etrusker,
aus einem Toten, den ein Raum empfing,

what's free only in its reflection,
darkened by us. Or that an animal, mute,
looks up and calmly looks through us.
This we call fate: to stand opposite
and nothing else and forever opposite.

If consciousness like ours existed in that
confident animal heading toward us
from another direction—, it would whip us round
in its wake. But for the animal,
its being is infinite, unfettered, unconcerned
with its own condition, pure as its outward gaze.
And where we see future, it sees everything,
and itself in everything, forever healed.

And yet in the watchful, warm animal is
the weight and care of a deep sadness.
For what so often overwhelms us
adheres in the animal as well,—a memory,
as if all that we seek
had been closer once, more true, its ties to us
infinitely tender. Here all is separation,
there it was breath. After the first home, the second
seems a hybrid place, wind-blown.
   O bliss of the tiny creature who
remains forever in the womb that bore it:
O happiness of the gnat, who still leaps *within*,
even on its wedding-day: for womb is all.
And see the half-assurance of the bird,
who by birth almost knows both worlds,
as if it were a soul of the Etruscans,
freed from a dead person, and received in a new space,

doch mit der ruhenden Figur als Deckel.
Und wie bestürzt ist eins, das fliegen muß
und stammt aus einem Schoß. Wie vor sich selbst
erschreckt, durchzuckts die Luft, wie wenn ein Sprung
durch eine Tasse geht. So reißt die Spur
der Fledermaus durchs Porzellan des Abends.

Und wir: Zuschauer, immer, überall,
dem allen zugewandt und nie hinaus!
Uns überfüllts. Wir ordnens. Es zerfällt.
Wir ordnens wieder und zerfallen selbst.

Wer hat uns also umgedreht, daß wir,
was wir auch tun, in jener Haltung sind
von einem, welcher fortgeht? Wie er auf
dem letzten Hügel, der ihm ganz sein Tal
noch einmal zeigt, sich wendet, anhält, weilt—,
so leben wir und nehmen immer Abschied.

but with the same reclining figure as the lid.
And how crestfallen is the womb-born creature
who has to fly. As if startled
by itself, it zigzags though the air, like a crack
through a cup. So the tracery of a bat
rends the porcelain of evening.

And we: spectators, always, everywhere,
facing all this, never the beyond.
It overfills us. We arrange it. It falls apart.
We arrange it again, and fall apart ourselves.

Who has turned us around like this, so that
whatever we do, we find ourselves in the attitude
of someone going away? Just as that person
on the last hill, which shows him his whole valley
one last time, turns, stops, lingers—,
so we live, forever taking our leave.

DIE NEUNTE ELEGIE

Warum, wenn es angeht, also die Frist des Daseins
hinzubringen, als Lorbeer, ein wenig dunkler als alles
andere Grün, mit kleinen Wellen an jedem
Blattrand (wie eines Windes Lächeln)—: warum dann
Menschliches müssen—und, Schicksal vermeidend,
sich sehnen nach Schicksal? . . .

                       Oh, *nicht*, weil Glück *ist*,
dieser voreilige Vorteil eines nahen Verlusts.
Nicht aus Neugier, oder zur Übung des Herzens,
das auch im Lorbeer *wäre*. . . . .

Aber weil Hiersein viel ist, und weil uns scheinbar
alles das Hiesige braucht, dieses Schwindende, das
seltsam uns angeht. Uns, die Schwindendsten. *Ein* Mal
jedes, nur *ein* Mal. *Ein* Mal und nichtmehr. Und wir auch
ein Mal. Nie wieder. Aber dieses
ein Mal gewesen zu sein, wenn auch nur *ein* Mal:
irdisch gewesen zu sein, scheint nicht widerrufbar.

Und so drängen wir uns und wollen es leisten,
wollens enthalten in unsern einfachen Händen,
im überfüllteren Blick und im sprachlosen Herzen.
Wollen es werden.—Wem es geben? Am liebsten
alles behalten für immer . . . Ach, in den andern Bezug,
wehe, was nimmt man hinüber? Nicht das Anschaun, das hier
langsam erlernte, und kein hier Ereignetes. Keins.
Also die Schmerzen. Also vor allem das Schwersein,
also der Liebe lange Erfahrung,—also
lauter Unsägliches. Aber später,

THE NINTH ELEGY

Why, if our time on earth could be
spent as laurel, its green darker than
all others, its leaves edged with
little waves (like the smile of a wind)—: then why do we
have to be human—and, avoiding destiny,
long for destiny? . . .

Oh not because there is happiness,
that rash profit taken just prior to impending loss,
Not out of curiosity, or to give the heart practice,
reasons that would hold for the laurel too. . . . .

But because being here is so much, and because everything
in this fleeting world seems to need us, and
strangely speaks to us. Us, the most fleeting. Once
for everything, only once. Once and no more. And we, too,
only once. Never again. But to have been,
this once, if only this once:
to have been *of the earth* can never be taken back.

And so we drive ourselves, and want to achieve it,
want to contain it all in our simple hands,
our more overcrowded gaze, our speechless heart.
Want to become it.—And give it, to whom? Best of all,
hold on to all of it forever . . . Ah, but into that other relation,
what can we carry over? Not the power to see, learned here
so slowly, and none of the things that happened here. Not one.
The pain, then. Above all the sadness,
and the long experience of love,—only
what is unsayable. But later,

unter den Sternen, was solls: *die* sind *besser* unsäglich.
Bringt doch der Wanderer auch vom Hange des Bergrands
nicht eine Hand voll Erde ins Tal, die Allen unsägliche,
     sondern
ein erworbenes Wort, reines, den gelben und blaun
Enzian. Sind wir vielleicht *hier,* um zu sagen: Haus,
Brücke, Brunnen, Tor, Krug, Obstbaum, Fenster,—
höchstens: Säule, Turm .... aber zu *sagen,* verstehs,
oh zu sagen *so,* wie selber die Dinge niemals
innig meinten zu sein. Ist nicht die heimliche List
dieser verschwiegenen Erde, wenn sie die Liebenden drängt,
daß sich in ihrem Gefühl jedes und jedes entzückt?
Schwelle: was ists für zwei
Liebende, daß sie die eigne ältere Schwelle der Tür
ein wenig verbrauchen, auch sie, nach den vielen vorher
und vor den Künftigen . . . . , leicht.

Hier ist des *Säglichen* Zeit, *hier* seine Heimat.
Sprich und bekenn. Mehr als je
fallen die Dinge dahin, die erlebbaren, denn,
was sie verdrängend ersetzt, ist ein Tun ohne Bild.
Tun unter Krusten, die willig zerspringen, sobald
innen das Handeln entwächst und sich anders begrenzt.
Zwischen den Hämmern besteht
unser Herz, wie die Zunge
zwischen den Zähnen, die doch,
dennoch, die preisende bleibt.

Preise dem Engel die Welt, nicht die unsägliche, *ihm*
kannst du nicht großtun mit herrlich Erfühltem; im Weltall,

among the stars, what good is it: there they are *better* unsaid.
For the wanderer doesn't bring back from the mountainside
to the valley a handful of earth, unsayable to everyone, but
rather a word gained, a pure word, the yellow and blue
gentian. Are we perhaps here in order to say: house,
bridge, fountain, gate, pitcher, fruit tree, window,—
at most: column, tower . . . . but to say, you understand,
oh, to say them as even the things themselves
never meant so inwardly to be. Isn't this the devious cunning
of our reticent earth when it urges lovers on:
that in their emotion each and every thing would delight in
        itself?
Threshold: what does it mean to two
lovers when they wear away a little their own older threshold,
they too, after the many before,
before those to come . . . . lightly.

Here is the time for the sayable, *here* its home.
Speak and avow it. More than ever
things that can be experienced fall away,
shunted aside and superseded by unseeable acts,
acts under crusts that readily shatter
when the inner workings outgrow them and seek new
        containment.
Between the hammers
our heart endures, like the tongue
between the teeth, which yet
continues to praise.

Praise this world to the angel, not the unsayable one,
you won't impress him with your glorious emotions; out there,

wo er fühlender fühlt, bist du ein Neuling. Drum zeig
ihm das Einfache, das, von Geschlecht zu Geschlechtern
    gestaltet,
als ein Unsriges lebt, neben der Hand und im Blick.
Sag ihm die Dinge. Er wird staunender stehn; wie du standest
bei dem Seiler in Rom, oder beim Töpfer am Nil.
Zeig ihm, wie glücklich ein Ding sein kann, wie schuldlos
    und unser,
wie selbst das klagende Leid rein zur Gestalt sich entschließt,
dient als ein Ding, oder stirbt in ein Ding—, und jenseits
selig der Geige entgeht.—Und diese, von Hingang
lebenden Dinge verstehn, daß du sie rühmst; vergänglich,
traun sie ein Rettendes uns, den Vergänglichsten, zu.
Wollen, wir sollen sie ganz im unsichtbarn Herzen verwandeln
in—o unendlich—in uns! Wer wir am Ende auch seien.

Erde, ist es nicht dies, was du willst: *unsichtbar*
in uns erstehn?—Ist es dein Traum nicht,
einmal unsichtbar zu sein?—Erde! unsichtbar!
Was, wenn Verwandlung nicht, ist dein drängender Auftrag?
Erde, du liebe, ich will. Oh glaub, es bedürfte
nicht deiner Frühlinge mehr, mich dir zu gewinnen—, *einer*,
ach, ein einziger ist schon dem Blute zu viel.
Namenlos bin ich zu dir entschlossen, von weit her.
Immer warst du im Recht, und dein heiliger Einfall
ist der vertrauliche Tod.

Siehe, ich lebe. Woraus? Weder Kindheit noch Zukunft
werden weniger . . . . . Überzähliges Dasein
entspringt mir im Herzen.

where he feels with more feeling, you're but a novice. Rather
    show him
some common thing, shaped through the generations,
that lives as ours, near to our hand and in our sight.
Tell him of things. He'll stand more awed; as you did
beside the ropemaker in Rome or the potter by the Nile.
Show him how joyful, how pure, how much ours, a thing
    can be,
how even the lamenting of sorrow resolves into pure form,
serves as a thing, or dies into a thing—, and, in going across,
blissfully flows from the violin.—And these things,
that live by going away, know that you praise them; fleeting,
they look to us for rescue, us, the most fleeting of all.
They want us to transform them completely in our invisible heart
into—oh infinitely—into ourselves. Whoever finally we will be.

Earth, isn't this what you want: to arise
in us *invisible*?—Isn't your dream
one day to be invisible?—Earth! invisible!
What if not transformation is your urgent commission?
Earth, my dearest, I will. Oh believe me, no more
of your springtimes are needed to win me over—, *one*,
a single one, already is too much for my blood.
Secretly, from afar, I have chosen you.
You have always been right and your most sacred thought
is intimate death.

Look, I'm alive. On what? Neither childhood nor future
grows less. . . . . Overabundant being
wells up in my heart.

DIE ZEHNTE ELEGIE

Daß ich dereinst, an dem Ausgang der grimmigen Einsicht,
Jubel und Ruhm aufsinge zustimmenden Engeln.
Daß von den klar geschlagenen Hämmern des Herzens
keiner versage an weichen, zweifelnden oder
reißenden Saiten. Daß mich mein strömendes Antlitz
glänzender mache; daß das unscheinbare Weinen
blühe. O wie werdet ihr dann, Nächte, mir lieb sein,
gehärmte. Daß ich euch knieender nicht, untröstliche
    Schwestern,
hinnahm, nicht in euer gelöstes
Haar mich gelöster ergab. Wir, Vergeuder der Schmerzen.
Wie wir sie absehn voraus, in die traurige Dauer,
ob sie nicht enden vielleicht. Sie aber sind ja
unser winterwähriges Laub, unser dunkeles Sinngrün,
eine der Zeiten des heimlichen Jahres—, nicht nur
Zeit—, sind Stelle, Siedelung, Lager, Boden, Wohnort.

Freilich, wehe, wie fremd sind die Gassen der Leid-Stadt,
wo in der falschen, aus Übertönung gemachten
Stille, stark, aus der Gußform des Leeren der Ausguß
prahlt: der vergoldete Lärm, das platzende Denkmal.
O, wie spurlos zerträte ein Engel ihnen den Trostmarkt,
den die Kirche begrenzt, ihre fertig gekaufte:
reinlich und zu und enttäuscht wie ein Postamt am Sonntag.
Draußen aber kräuseln sich immer die Ränder von Jahrmarkt.
Schaukeln der Freiheit! Taucher und Gaukler des Eifers!
Und des behübschten Glücks figürliche Schießstatt,

THE TENTH ELEGY

Let me, one day, emerging from this grim vision,
sing jubilation and praise to assenting angels.
Let not one clear-struck hammer of my heart
fail to sound from slack, doubting, or
breaking strings. Let my streaming face
make me more shining; let my simple tears
flower. How dear will you be to me then,
you nights of affliction. Why couldn't I kneel more deeply
    and accept you,
inconsolable sisters, or lose myself more
freely in your loosened hair. We spendthrifts of sorrows.
How we scan beyond them ahead into sad duration
to see if perhaps they might have an end. But they are truly
our winter-hardy foliage, the dark green of our life's meaning,
one season of our secret year—, not only
time—, but also place, settlement, shelter, soil, abode.

But, oh, how alien are the streets of the grief-city,
where, in the false silence, noise muffled by louder
noise, a casting from the mold of emptiness
boasts forth: gilded clamor, bursting memorial. Oh, how without
trace an angel would trample out their market of solace,
that abuts the church that they bought ready made:
tidy, shuttered, downcast, like a post office on Sunday.
But, farther out, the edges of the carnival billow.
Swings of freedom! Divers and jugglers of zeal!
And the tasty bliss of a figured shooting-gallery

wo es zappelt von Ziel und sich blechern benimmt,
wenn ein Geschickterer trifft. Von Beifall zu Zufall
taumelt er weiter; denn Buden jeglicher Neugier
werben, trommeln und plärrn. Für Erwachsene aber
ist noch besonders zu sehn, wie das Geld sich vermehrt,
    anatomisch,
nicht zur Belustigung nur: der Geschlechtsteil des Gelds,
alles, das Ganze, der Vorgang—, das unterrichtet und macht
fruchtbar . . . .
. . . . Oh aber gleich darüber hinaus,
hinter der letzten Planke, beklebt mit Plakaten des >Todlos<,
jenes bitteren Biers, das den Trinkenden süß scheint,
wenn sie immer dazu frische Zerstreuungen kaun . . . ,
gleich im Rücken der Planke, gleich dahinter, ists *wirklich*.
Kinder spielen, und Liebende halten einander,—abseits,
ernst, im ärmlichen Gras, und Hunde haben Natur.
Weiter noch zieht es den Jüngling; vielleicht, daß er eine
    junge
Klage liebt . . . . . Hinter ihr her kommt er in Wiesen. Sie sagt:
—Weit. Wir wohnen dort draußen . . . .
                                        Wo? Und der Jüngling
folgt. Ihn rührt ihre Haltung. Die Schulter, der Hals—,
    vielleicht
ist sie von herrlicher Herkunft. Aber er läßt sie, kehrt um,
wendet sich, winkt . . . Was solls? Sie ist eine Klage.

Nur die jungen Toten, im ersten Zustand
zeitlosen Gleichmuts, dem der Entwöhnung,
folgen ihr liebend. Mädchen

where targets spin and clang tinnily
when a better shot hits. From cheers to chance
he lurches: booths catering to every taste
bark, drum, blare. But there's still one show,
a must-see, for adults only, how money reproduces,
anatomically, and not just for entertainment: money's genitals,
everything, the works, the act itself—, it's instructional and
     improves your
virility . . . .
. . . . Oh, but just beyond it,
behind the billboards pasted up with posters for "Deathless,"
that bitter beer tasting sweet to the drinkers
provided they keep chewing on a new distraction . . . ,
there at your back, right behind the billboard, is the real
     world.
Children play, and couples hold each other,—off to the side,
it gets more serious, on the patchy grass, and dogs do what is
     natural.
The youth is led on further still; perhaps he's in love with
a young lament. . . . . . He goes with her into the meadow. She
     says:
"Far away. We live out there. . . ."
                         "Where?" And the young man
follows. Her bearing stirs him. Her shoulders, her neck—,
"Perhaps she's of noble origin." But he lets her go,
looks after her and waves . . . "What's the use? She's a lament."
Only those who died young, who are in their first stage
of timeless serenity, a period of dehabituation from the world,
lovingly follow her. She waits for

wartet sie ab und befreundet sie. Zeigt ihnen leise,
was sie an sich hat. Perlen des Leids und die feinen
Schleier der Duldung.—Mit Jünglingen geht sie
schweigend.

Aber dort, wo sie wohnen, im Tal, der Älteren eine, der
    Klagen,
nimmt sich des Jünglinges an, wenn er fragt:—Wir waren,
sagt sie, ein Großes Geschlecht, einmal, wir Klagen. Die
    Väter
trieben den Bergbau dort in dem großen Gebirg; bei
    Menschen
findest du manchmal ein Stück geschliffenes Ur-Leid
oder, aus altem Vulkan, schlackig versteinerten Zorn.
Ja, das stammte von dort. Einst waren wir reich.—

Und sie leitet ihn leicht durch die weite Landschaft der
    Klagen,
zeigt ihm die Säulen der Tempel oder die Trümmer
jener Burgen, von wo Klage-Fürsten das Land
einstens weise beherrscht. Zeigt ihm die hohen
Tränenbäume und Felder blühender Wehmut,
(Lebendige kennen sie nur als sanftes Blattwerk);
zeigt ihm die Tiere der Trauer, weidend,—und manchmal
schreckt ein Vogel und zieht, flach ihnen fliegend durchs
    Aufschaun,
weithin das schriftliche Bild seines vereinsamten Schreis.—
Abends führt sie ihn hin zu den Gräbern der Alten
aus dem Klage-Geschlecht, den Sibyllen und Warn-Herrn.
Naht aber Nacht, so wandeln sie leiser, und bald
mondets empor, das über Alles

the girls and befriends them. Gently shows them
what she has on. Pearls of sorrow, delicate
veils of forbearance.—With the youths she walks
saying nothing.

But there, in the valley where they live, an elder lament
attends to the youth's questions: "We were once,"
she says, "a great clan, we laments. Our forefathers
worked mines up in those tall mountains; among humans
occasionally a cut stone of primal sorrow turns up,
or a slag of petrified wrath from an ancient volcano.
Yes, those came from up there. We were rich once."

And lightly she leads him through the vast landscape of
        laments,
shows him columns from the temples, or the ruins
of those castles from which Princes of Lament
once wisely ruled the land. Shows him the lofty
trees of tears and the fields of blossoming sorrow,
(known to the living only as soft foliage);
shows him the animals of mourning, grazing,—and from
        time to time
a startled bird, flying low through their upward gaze,
scripts into the distance the image of its solitary cry.—
At dusk she shows him the graves of the elders
of the House of Lament, the sibyls and dire prophets.
As night draws near, they stroll more quietly, and soon
the sepulchre rises moonlike before them, watching over

wachende Grab-Mal. Brüderlich jenem am Nil,
der erhabene Sphinx—: der verschwiegenen Kammer
Antlitz.
Und sie staunen dem krönlichen Haupt, das für immer,
schweigend, der Menschen Gesicht
auf die Waage der Sterne gelegt.

Nicht erfaßt es sein Blick, im Frühtod
schwindelnd. Aber ihr Schaun,
hinter dem Pschent-Rand hervor, scheucht es die Eule. Und
    sie,
streifend im langsamen Abstrich die Wange entlang,
jene der reifesten Rundung,
zeichnet weich in das neue
Totengehör, über ein doppelt
aufgeschlagenes Blatt, den unbeschreiblichen Umriß.

Und höher, die Sterne. Neue. Die Sterne des Leidlands.
Langsam nennt sie die Klage:—Hier,
siehe: den *Reiter*, den *Stab*, und das vollere Sternbild
nennen sie: *Fruchtkranz*. Dann, weiter, dem Pol zu:
Wiege; Weg; Das Brennende Buch; Puppe; Fenster.
Aber im südlichen Himmel, rein wie im Innern
einer gesegneten Hand, das klar erglänzende >M<,
das die Mütter bedeutet . . . . . .—

Doch der Tote muß fort, und schweigend bringt ihn die
    ältere
Klage bis an die Talschlucht,
wo es schimmert im Mondschein:
die Quelle der Freude. In Ehrfurcht

everything. Like a brother to the one on the Nile,
the sublime Sphinx—: the face of the hidden
burial chamber.
And they marvel at its crownlike head, which forever
silently placed the human face
on the scales of the stars.

He can't take it all in, dazed
from early death. But their looking
flushes an owl from behind the rim of the crown. And
brushing downwards slowly along the great cheek,
the one of ripest roundness,
the bird limns into the dead youth's new
hearing, across a double
open page, the indescribable contour.

And, higher, the stars. New stars. Of the grief-land.
Slowly the lament names them: "Look, there:
the *Rider*, the *Staff*; that fuller constellation is called:
Garland of Fruit. Over there, more toward the Pole:
Cradle; Path; The Burning Book; Puppet; Window.
In the southern sky, pure as in the palm
of a blessed hand, just starting to sparkle, the '*M*'
standing for Mothers . . . . ."

But the dead one must go on; the elder
lament brings him, in silence, up to the gorge,
which shimmers in moonlight:
the Source of Joy. She says the name

nennt sie sie, sagt:——Bei den Menschen
ist sie ein tragender Strom.——

Stehn am Fuß des Gebirgs.
Und da umarmt sie ihn, weinend.

Einsam steigt er dahin, in die Berge des Ur-Leids.
Und nicht einmal sein Schritt klingt aus dem tonlosen Los.

*

Aber erweckten sie uns, die unendlich Toten, ein Gleichnis,
siehe, sie zeigten vielleicht auf die Kätzchen der leeren
Hasel, die hängenden, oder
meinten den Regen, der fällt auf dunkles Erdreich im
    Frühjahr.——

Und wir, die an *steigendes* Glück
denken, empfänden die Rührung,
die uns beinah bestürzt,
wenn ein Glückliches *fällt*.

reverently, and adds: "Down among humans
it's a 'carrying' river."

They stand at the foot of the mountain.
Tearfully, she embraces him.

He climbs on alone, into the mountains of primal sorrow.
No step rings back from that soundless fate.

*

But if they, the infinitely dead, were awakening an image
    within us,
see, they would perhaps point to the catkins
hanging from the bare hazels, or
mean the rain pelting the dark earth in spring.—

And we, who think of happiness as
rising, would feel an emotion
that almost startles
when a happy thing *falls*.

from THE SONNETS TO ORPHEUS

I , 2

Und fast ein Mädchen wars und ging hervor
aus diesem einigen Glück von Sang und Leier
und glänzte klar durch ihre Frühlingsschleier
und machte sich ein Bett in meinem Ohr.

Und schlief in mir. Und alles war ihr Schlaf.
Die Bäume, die ich je bewundert, diese
fühlbare Ferne, die gefühlte Wiese
und jedes Staunen, das mich selbst betraf.

Sie schlief die Welt. Singender Gott, wie hast
du sie vollendet, daß sie nicht begehrte,
erst wach zu sein? Sieh, sie erstand und schlief.

Wo ist ihr Tod? O, wirst du dies Motiv
erfinden noch, eh sich dein Lied verzehrte?—
Wo sinkt sie hin aus mir? . . . Ein Mädchen fast. . . .

And almost a girl it was who was born
from this happy union of song and lyre
and gleamed clearly through her springtime veils
and made herself a bed in my ear.

And slept in me. And all things were her sleep.
The trees I have ever held in awe, this
feelable farness, the felt meadow,
and every astonishment ever concerning me.

She slept the world. Singing god, how did
you make her so complete that she didn't desire
first to be awake? See, she arose and slept.

Where is her death? Oh, will you yet invent
this motif before your song consumes itself?—
Where does she sink to out of me? . . . A girl almost. . . .

I , 3

Ein Gott vermags. Wie aber, sag mir, soll
ein Mann ihm folgen durch die schmale Leier?
Sein Sinn ist Zwiespalt. An der Kreuzung zweier
Herzwege steht kein Tempel für Apoll.

Gesang, wie du ihn lehrst, ist nicht Begehr,
nicht Werbung um ein endlich noch Erreichtes;
Gesang ist Dasein. Für den Gott ein Leichtes.
Wann aber *sind* wir? Und wann wendet *er*

an unser Sein die Erde und die Sterne?
Dies *ists* nicht, Jüngling, daß du liebst, wenn auch
die Stimme dann den Mund dir aufstößt,—lerne

vergessen, daß du aufsangst. Das verrinnt.
In Wahrheit singen, ist ein andrer Hauch.
Ein Hauch um nichts. Ein Wehn im Gott. Ein Wind.

A god can do it. But tell me how a man
is to follow through the narrow lyre?
His mind is cleft. No temple for Apollo
stands where two heart-ways cross.

Song, as you teach it, is not desire,
not suing for a thing at last attained;
song is existence. Easy, for the god.
But when do we *exist*? And when will *he*

turn toward us the earth and the stars?
It's not, young man, when you're in love, even if
then your voice thrusts open your mouth,—learn

to forget you once lifted yourself in song. That doesn't last.
True singing is a different kind of breath.
A breath about nothing. A blowing in the god. A wind.

I , 5

Errichtet keinen Denkstein. Laßt die Rose
nur jedes Jahr zu seinen Gunsten blühn.
Denn Orpheus ists. Seine Metamorphose
in dem und dem. Wir sollen uns nicht mühn

um andre Namen. Ein für alle Male
ists Orpheus, wenn es singt. Er kommt und geht.
Ists nicht schon viel, wenn er die Rosenschale
um ein paar Tage manchmal übersteht?

O wie er schwinden muß, daß ihrs begrifft!
Und wenn ihm selbst auch bangte, daß er schwände.
Indem sein Wort das Hiersein übertrifft,

ist er schon dort, wohin ihrs nicht begleitet.
Der Leier Gitter zwängt ihm nicht die Hände.
Und er gehorcht, indem er überschreitet.

I , 5

Erect no memorial. Just let the rose
bloom each year to his benefit.
For it is Orpheus. His metamorphosis
is this and this. No need to trouble ourselves with

other names. Now and forever,
it is Orpheus, when there's singing. He comes and goes.
Isn't it enough if sometimes he overstays
even by only a few days the bowl of roses?

O how he must vanish, to make you understand!
even if he take fright at the vanishing.
Whenever his word goes beyond our being here,

he is already there, where you do not follow.
His hands are not held down by the strings of the lyre.
And he obeys, in that he oversteps.

I , 1 9

Wandelt sich rasch auch die Welt
wie Wolkengestalten,
alles Vollendete fällt
heim zum Uralten.

Über dem Wandel und Gang,
weiter und freier,
währt noch dein Vor-Gesang,
Gott mit der Leier.

Nicht sind die Leiden erkannt,
nicht ist die Liebe gelernt,
und was im Tod uns entfernt,

ist nicht entschleiert.
Einzig das Lied überm Land
heiligt und feiert.

Though the world changes quickly,
like shapes of clouds,
everything once finished falls
back to ancient ground.

Far above change and progress,
wider and more free,
your early song still persists,
god with the lyre.

Suffering has not been understood,
love has not been learned,
and what goes from us in death

is not revealed.
Over the land song alone
hallows and celebrates.

II, 13

Sei allem Abschied voran, als wäre er hinter
dir, wie der Winter, der eben geht.
Denn unter Wintern ist einer so endlos Winter,
daß, überwinternd, dein Herz überhaupt übersteht.

Sei immer tot in Eurydike—, singender steige,
preisender steige zurück in den reinen Bezug.
Hier, unter Schwindenden, sei, im Reiche der Neige,
sei ein klingendes Glas, das sich im Klang schon zerschlug.

Sei—und wisse zugleich des Nicht-Seins Bedingung,
den unendlichen Grund deiner innigen Schwingung,
daß du sie völlig vollziehst dieses einzige Mal.

Zu dem gebrauchten sowohl, wie zum dumpfen und stummen
Vorrat der vollen Natur, den unsäglichen Summen,
zähle dich jubelnd hinzu und vernichte die Zahl.

Anticipate all parting, as if it were behind
you, like the winter that's now passing.
For under winters is one winter so endless,
only in overwintering can your heart overcome.

Be dead forever in Eurydice—, sing and step back,
praise and step back into pure relation.
Here, among the vanishing, in this realm of decline,
be the ringing glass that shattered of its own sound.

Be—and know, too, the condition of not-being,
endless source of your inmost vibration,
and this one time you have, bring it to completion.

Then to the used-up, as well as the dull and mute
stores of full nature, those countless quantities,
add yourself, exulting, and strike the count.